100760

P9-DTM-156

HUSBANDS, WIVES, PARENTS, CHILDREN

Husbands, Wives, Parents, Children

Foundations for the Christian Family

Ralph Martin

Servant Books
Ann Arbor, Michigan

Copyright © 1978 by Ralph Martin

Published by Servant Books
P.O. Box 8617
Ann Arbor, Michigan 48107

Available from Servant Books
Distribution Center
237 N. Michigan
South Bend, Indiana 46601

ISBN 0-89283-050-6 (paperback)
ISBN 0-89283-051-4 (hardback)

Printed in the United States of America

Unless otherwise indicated, Scripture quotations are from
the Revised Standard Version, copyright 1946, 1952,
© 1971, 1973 by the Division of Christian Education of
the National Council of the Churches of Christ in the
U.S.A. Used by permission.

The initials NAB indicate that a Scripture quotation has
been taken from The New American Bible, copyright 1970
by the Confraternity of Christian Doctrine, Washington,
D.C.

+8.4
A 365h

L.I.F.E. College Library
1100 Glendale Blvd.
Los Angeles, Calif. 90026

Acknowledgments

The writing of this book began in 1973, when I met with Jim Cavnar, Ron Ghormley, Chris Graulich, Jim McFadden, and Tony Redente in order to prepare a course on Christian family life. We ranged in age from twenty-four to forty-four, and could draw on a collective experience of raising children through every stage of development. The course which eventually developed from our meetings was designed for couples experiencing a renewed Christian life in our ecumenical community in Ann Arbor, Michigan. It has since been used by many Christian groups, and it is the foundation for this book.

Experience being the best teacher, it is to my wife Anne and our three children—John, Mary Sarah, and Elizabeth Anne—that I owe most of my own knowledge of family life. I also owe a debt of gratitude to those who have shared closely in our family life, especially Maureen Moreau, Mary Ann Jahr, Michael Jahr, Tony and Julie Anne Redente, and Randy and Theresa Cirner. They have given Anne and me many insights into our responsibilities as parents. And of course, my own parents, in their continuing example of Christian love and faithfulness, have contributed in more ways than I could analyze.

I want to acknowledge the special contribution of Gary and Barbara Morgan, who have given my wife and me much support by sharing their own struggles and victories as a married couple. Gary and Barbara have made a substantial contribution to this book, and it is to Barbara that I owe much of the chapter directed to Christian wives.

Finally, I would like to acknowledge the substantial

027413

editorial help of Nick Cavnar, who has sometimes taken very rough material from me and made it readable. This book would have been even longer in the making had Nick not lent his abilities. I also want to thank Martha Gebhart for her help in copyediting and proofreading the text and assembling the index.

This book is dedicated to all my married brothers and sisters who are striving to follow the Lord's ways in the life of their families. May we all be blessed and helped by him in our task.

Brussels, February, 1978

027413

CONTENTS

Blessed is everyone who fears the Lord,
    who walks in his ways!
You shall eat the fruit of the labor of
    your hands;
you shall be happy, and it shall be well
    with you.
Your wife will be like a fruitful vine
    within your house;
your children will be like olive shoots
    around your table.
Lo, thus shall the man be blessed who
    fears the Lord.

Psalm 128:1-4

Part One

Husbands and Wives

CHAPTER ONE

PRESSURES ON THE CHRISTIAN FAMILY

Not too long ago, I was talking to a young married man about the responsibilities of raising children in the Lord.

"You know," he said to me, "It doesn't seem to me that my grandparents paid all this much attention to raising their children, yet they turned out to be good Christians. Is that just my imagination, or is it actually harder to raise Christian children these days?"

"No, it's not your imagination," I told him. "It really is harder to raise children as Christians. In fact, everything about Christian family life is getting harder."

Even one generation ago, our Western societies provided many supports that made it easier for a family to live and grow as Christians. Today most of these supports have disappeared, and society's attitudes toward marriage and family have shifted in directions totally opposed to Christian principles. We can see it all around us in rising divorce rates, alienation between children and parents, rejection of marriage and family structures, and antagonism toward having children.

This change in social attitudes has a big effect on Christian families. We can look at what is happening with divorce, for one example. A hundred years ago, most Western societies still held to the Christian view of marriage as a monogamous, life-long relationship. Where divorce was even permitted, it was considered an extreme solution valid only in the most intolerable situations. This is not to say that all marriages a hundred years ago were ideal Christian relationships; only that general social attitudes did support a Christian understanding of the marriage commitment.

Today, however, a full twenty-five to thirty percent of all new marriages end in divorce. With this rise in numbers has come a more relaxed attitude toward divorce. Society now regards divorce as a reasonable option for a marriage that becomes dull or unrewarding. A Christian couple who want to hold their marriage together through hard times have trouble doing so today, because the attractive presentation of divorce creates a subtle pressure to break up.

Sociological and historical studies point to many factors behind the shift in attitudes toward marriage and family. The development of a technological culture, the trend to urban living, and the dominance of capitalism have all contributed to a broad change in social thinking, a change characterized by an overriding emphasis on individual fulfillment. Where society was once concerned to protect various social units—including the family—its main concern now is to let each individual pursue the goal of self-fulfillment, even at the cost of the common good.[1]

Naturally, this shift has important consequences for society's attitude toward the family unit. For example, recent American court decisions have deprived parents of any say in their daughter's decision to have an abortion—even if she is a minor. Clearly, this decision works to undermine the importance and authority of the family bond for the sake of what is seen as an individual right.

Another factor lies behind the current shift in social attitudes, one that is of even greater concern to Christians. That is the rapid secularization of Western culture. Where

1. A recent study of family history (*The Making of the Modern Family,* by Edward Shorter, Basic Books, 1975) documents this trend.

most Western societies once identified to at least some extent with Christian beliefs and values, they have now become almost completely secular. Our government institutions, schools and mass media can no longer be expected to support Christian life. Indeed they often prove actively hostile. More than a century ago, the German philosopher Friedrich Nietzsche predicted this trend. He wrote that Western society had already lost the foundation of active Christian faith, and that it would go on to strip itself of the last vestiges of that faith.

The de-Christianization of the West poses an enormous challenge to the Christian churches. No longer can they presume their members live in an environment that supports Christian life. No longer can they even presume that the beliefs, attitudes, and lifestyle of their members are authentically Christian. Vast numbers of people who remain Christian in name—who stay on the church rolls, attend occasional services, are baptized, married and buried in church—are most deeply influenced by the secular culture, not by the church. In France, for instance, large numbers of people who no longer hold to Christian faith or morality in daily life still regard themselves, perhaps sentimentally, as Catholics.

Yet the Christian people seem able to make only a mixed response to this great challenge. There are those Christians who want the churches simply to accept society's new directions, even when that means twisting the gospels a bit to ease the gap between Christ's teaching and the world's. If society accepts pre-marital sex, adultery, abortion, and homosexuality, they cannot see why the church has to keep calling them sins.

Other Christians are confused. They don't know who or what to believe; they do not clearly understand either Christianity or the society around them. They sometimes feel bitter about being in a situation that they cannot understand or deal with, but they do not know where to go for help.

Many more Christians are basically discouraged, even despairing. They grasp the truth of Christianity and want to live a Christian life, but find they are unable to live out their beliefs or transmit them to their children. They experience little or no help either from God or from the church. Often their discouragement breaks out in frustration or hostility directed toward themselves, their children, the church, even the Lord.

The three responses I have just described all share one element: a sense that the way of life taught in Scriptures and taught for centuries by the Christian church is no longer possible in today's society. Unless changes are made, that sense may be accurate. Unless Christians are able to face up to the pressures confronting them and reassess their relationship to contemporary culture, many will find themselves incapable of living the life demanded by the gospel. They must understand the basic elements of Christian life before they can recognize and resist forces that would destroy that life.

This is a weakness of some marriage renewal or enrichment programs now popular among Christians. They assume that the basic fabric of Christian marriage in our culture is still sound and only needs a little brushing up. These programs do achieve much good, but I doubt that they will prove equal to the real crisis facing the family. I believe that what we need at this point is an explicit and comprehensive effort to restore the very foundations of marriage in Christ, foundations that have been seriously weakened by the secularization of our society.

In this book, I hope to explain what those foundations are and to offer practical wisdom for the life of the modern Christian family. The particular realities of family life discussed here may not seem distinctively Christian—communication, sex, discipline of children. But the fact that these realities are to be lived out by men and women who are new creatures in Christ makes a tremendous difference. For example, look at the way the gospels speak about authority. Jesus contrasts the way authority is used in the world, where it is a way of lording it over others for one's own advantage, to the way authority is to operate among his people, where it is a means of service, of laying down one's life for the common good.

Some may at first glance misunderstand what I say about the realities of Christian marriage, and think that I am simply espousing a return to traditional family patterns of a hundred years ago. But I am not interested in a return simply to traditional lifestyles. The Victorian family of a hundred years ago was not necessarily any more authentically Christian than the secularized family of today. All human societies and traditions need to be constantly judged and purified by God's Word. What I am interested in is presenting the abiding principles of God's creative purposes—the teaching of Christ and the apostles as found in Scripture and handed down to us by the church.

I believe that the Lord has given us three supports that can help us both learn about and live out Christian family life. The first is an abiding, life-giving union with God's Word in Scripture and with the principles of faith maintained by the Christian people throughout their history. Too often today, scriptural instructions on family life or traditional Christian teaching on sexual morality is brushed off with the excuse that it was conditioned by the mistaken ideas of an earlier culture. The analytical techniques of modern scholarship, while important for determining the intended meaning of Scripture, can also be misused by exegetes most interested in finding a way around biblical truths that conflict with modern ideas.

I believe that if we approach Scripture with an attitude of humility, acknowledging its authority as God's revealed truth, we can find in it many practical lessons for how to live out our family commitments. However, seeking wisdom from Scripture is not something that each Christian family should do completely on its own. The best way to approach Scripture is in communion with the understanding handed down by the Christian people through many generations and in the context of a thriving local Christian community where one's insights and interpretations can be tested by those with more training in Scripture study and experience in the Christian life and faith.

My own use of Scripture reflects the study and prayerful discussion of many of my brothers and sisters of various Christian traditions. Due to the limited scope of this book, I will not go into all the exegetical questions involved in interpreting different passages. However, one of my colleagues, Stephen B. Clark, is now working on a book that will provide a detailed exegetical discussion of many passages that I use. I hope that his book will be available soon for those who want a further explanation of my use of Scripture.[2]

Personal union with God is the second vital element of Christian family life. All the good advice and communication techniques in the world will not revive Christian marriage unless we first come into a deeply committed relationship with the Father through the Lordship of Jesus. Christian marriage cannot exist apart from Christ. It is through our relationship with the Father and Jesus that we receive the gift of the Holy Spirit, the Counselor who is ready to lead, guide, strengthen, enlighten, encourage, and console us as we seek to live out God's Word. We need to approach our lives as married couples, as families, in obedient love and reverence for God, in total dedication to him and his ways.

A third element of Christian life is membership in the local body of believers, the Christian community. The Christian family is not meant to exist in a vacuum, but in the context of deeply committed relationships with those who are our brothers and sisters in Christ. Especially to-

---

2. The book, titled *Man and Woman in Christ,* is to be published by Servant Books.

day, when society as a whole rejects Christian values, we need strong, united communities that can provide a counter-environment to protect and support Christian growth.

I myself am a Roman Catholic who belongs to The Word of God, an ecumenical community centered in Ann Arbor, Michigan. More than seventeen hundred adults and children, representing almost every Christian tradition, make up our community. We all remain loyal members of our own churches at the same time that we belong to our ecumenical fellowship. Although I am now living in Europe, this community has contributed to many of the ideas presented in this book, and it has strengthened and supported the life of my family even while we have been overseas.

While I am a Roman Catholic, I have written this book for the use of Christians of a variety of denominations and traditions. I have tried both to establish foundational principles for the family and to offer practical advice, based on experience, on how to live out these principles in different circumstances.

This book is an attempt to speak to Christians in every situation about God's call to men and women in marriage. I want to examine that call as it is revealed in Scripture, then discuss how we can live it out with the help of the Spirit and the support of the Christian community. For I believe that it is only through dependence on these three realities that the Christian family can hope to flourish in a hostile world.

CHAPTER TWO

UNITY

T alk is cheap, the saying goes, and that seems particularly true when it comes to talk about unity. These days, every politician and popular singer apparently has to give at least an occasional plea for love and community and people getting together. If you listened to all the talk, you might well be convinced that some wonderful new age of harmony and peace is dawning for our whole society, only to be disappointed by the next day's headlines.

For behind the rhetoric, the real trend in today's society is not toward greater unity, but toward more and more individualism. This is, after all, the era that proclaims "do your own thing," that tells each individual to pursue an independent happiness without much concern for others. Some social commentators see so much preoccupation with self in our society that they call us "the new narcissists."

In the face of a society that encourages everyone to pursue a separate course, Jesus calls his people to unity, even to perfect unity. It was for Christians of today as much as of any time that he prayed: "May they all be one, as you, Father, are in me, and I in you; I pray that they may be one in us, that the world may believe that you sent me" (John 17:21).

The unity that Jesus desires for his disciples is not the insubstantial stuff of casual talk; it is as real and complete

as the unity that Jesus himself shares with his Father and
the Holy Spirit. It is a unity that welds separate individuals together into one body, able to move together under
the direction of one head. Jesus calls us to be in perfect
unity with one another and with him. He wants us to reflect in our relationships as sisters and brothers the same
unity that exists in the life of the Trinity.

The call to unity is addressed even more directly to
those Christians who are married. God intends the union
of husband and wife to embody in a special way the total
unity that he desires for all his people. He has designed
man and woman to fit together in marriage, to pass from
living as two separate individuals to a life as one body, one
flesh. Even our reproductive design reflects this purpose:
man and woman must unite to produce new life.

The book of Genesis emphasizes this fundamental intention when it describes the creation of man and woman.
The account begins with the creation of man alone: "the
Lord God formed man of dust from the ground, and
breathed into his nostrils the breath of life" (2:7). But
Genesis tells us that God was not satisfied with this solitary male: "It is not good that the man should be alone"
(2:18). Note the contrast here with the phrase that describes God's satisfaction when his creation is completed:
"And God saw everything that he had made, and behold, it
was very good" (1:31). Something about man by himself
was not good; he was incomplete, unfinished.

"So the Lord God caused a deep sleep to fall upon the
man, and while he slept took out one of his ribs and closed
up its place with flesh; and the rib which the Lord God had
taken from the man he made into a woman" (2:21-22).

Taken superficially, this passage might seem to belittle
women: "What do you mean, we got made out of someone's rib!" But Arab friends have told me that in their
culture a person often calls his closest friend his "rib." "Joe
down the block is my good friend, my rib." The word indi-

cates that two people are very close and share a genuine bond of unity.

In the same way, Genesis uses the image of the rib to show how closely man and woman are bound together. They are made of the same substance; they share the same life. Adam recognized this at once when he awoke and saw the woman: "This at last is bone of my bones and flesh of my flesh" (2:23).

That fundamental unity, we are told, is the reason why "a man leaves his father and mother and cleaves to his wife, and they become one flesh" (2:24). In the Lord's plan, a husband and wife do not just live together on friendly terms. They *cleave* to one another—one of the strongest possible words to apply to a human relationship—and become *one flesh*. While "one flesh" obviously refers to the physical union of sexual intercourse, it also means that husband and wife become a new social entity, a unit that works as one.

"The man and his wife were both naked and were not ashamed" (2:25). God's original plan for the union of man and woman included no shame or guilt or disorder. There was peace and freedom.

We know that this original unity, and the harmony that marked it, did not last. When men and women disrupted their relationship with God, they also disrupted the harmony between themselves. Genesis tells us that after the fall God said to the woman: "I will greatly multiply your pain in childbearing; in pain you shall bring forth children, yet your desire shall be for your husband, and he shall rule over you" (Gen. 3:16). To the man he said, "Cursed is the ground because of you; in toil shall you eat of it all the days of your life; thorns and thistles it shall bring forth to you; and you shall eat the plants of the field" (3:17-18).

What a change in the relationship of husband and wife! Where once unity and peace characterized their life together, now frustration and anxiety fill it. Even the new life that springs from their union causes the woman pain. The man, meanwhile, is caught in an endless, painful struggle to make a living.

As a sign of this change, the man and woman now have clothing. The freedom and rightness that once marked their relationship has vanished. In its place has entered a sense of shame.

Fallen humanity never fully recovered the ideal of married unity that God offered the first man and woman. Even among God's chosen people, divorce—the mark of a final breaking of unity—was a common occurence. As long as men and women were unable to restore their original union with God, they could not live up to God's design for their life together.

That is why Jesus' teaching is so important for our understanding of Christian marriage. According to the gospel of Matthew, some Pharisees tried to test Jesus by asking him: "Is it lawful to divorce one's wife for any cause?" (19:3). At the time, Jewish authorities were divided into two camps on this question: some allowed divorce only on very strict grounds, others advocated more leniency. The Pharisees wanted Jesus to come down on one side or the other of the question so that he would antagonize half the people.

But Jesus' answer went beyond what the Pharisees probably expected. "Have you not read that he who made them from the beginning made them male and female, and said, 'For this reason a man shall leave his father and mother and be joined to his wife, and the two shall become one flesh'? So they are no longer two but one flesh. What therefore God has joined together, let not man put asunder" (19:4-6).

"The two shall become one flesh." With these words, Jesus reaffirms in the new covenant God's original plan for marriage. He tells us that husband and wife actually do become one unit, one flesh, and that God himself stands behind their union. God wills full union between them as a fundamental part of his plan and creation. Jesus allows no room for compromise on this issue, stating even more bluntly that "whoever divorces his wife ... and marries another, commits adultery, and he who marries a divorced woman commits adultery" (19:9).

The gospel of Matthew, although not the other gospels that record this incident, allows a qualification to this statement: "except for unchastity" (19:9). The interpretation of that passage has caused considerable controversy, and various Christian denominations now take quite different stances on permitting divorce. But for many centuries the church took a very strict position on divorce in keeping with Scripture.

I realize the plight of the many divorced Christians today, and I do not want to imply any judgment on their individual situations. That is up to the Lord and to the responsible authorities in the churches. Today, when so many people who marry in church are only nominally Christian, one can even question whether some partners actually contract a Christian marriage.

But the complexities of the divorce question should not distract us from the clear scriptural teaching that God wants the unity of husband and wife to remain unbroken. The book of Genesis tells us that this was his original intention, and the gospels reaffirm that ideal for the Christian people. Its reaffirmation was anticipated in the Old Testament by the prophet Malachi, who said, " ... the Lord is witness between you and the wife of your youth ... she is your companion, your betrothed wife. Did he not make one being, with flesh and spirit? ... You must then safeguard life that is your own, and not break faith with the wife of your youth. For I hate divorce, says the Lord, the God of Israel" (Mal. 2:14-16 NAB).

Paul came later to realize the full significance of the

unbroken unity of marriage, saying, "This is a great foreshadowing; I mean that it refers to Christ and the church" (Eph. 5:32 NAB). The fidelity of husband and wife is a sign of God's unbroken covenant love for his people. That is one reason why God insists on the unity of Christian marriage; he wants marriage to reflect his love and his life, to set before the world an image of his own relationship to the body of Christ.

CHAPTER THREE

IS UNITY POSSIBLE?

When Jesus' disciples understood what he was saying about the indissolubility of marriage, they told him: "If such is the case of a man with his wife, it is not expedient to marry" (Matt. 19:10). The ideal of life-long unity with no option for divorce seemed to them, as it seems to many today, far too difficult to be possible. Perhaps for fallen humanity such perfect, unbroken unity is impossible. Yet the fact remains that we have been designed by our Creator to live in that kind of permanent covenant relationship. Just as Jesus can restore us to our original unity with God, so he can restore to us our unity as husband and wife.

In the same chapter of Matthew's gospel, Jesus responds to another objection to one of his statements by saying: "With men it is impossible, but with God all things are possible" (19:26). Jesus is giving us a high ideal for married life, and he tells us, "You can't do it by yourself. You need the power of God." It is Jesus himself and his body who can provide the power and wisdom we need.

I believe that Jesus offers us three supports within marriage itself that make full unity possible: a personal relationship with him, a relationship to each other as Christian brother and sister, and the principle of Christian governmental authority. (The support of the larger Christian community is also important, and will be discussed in a later chapter.)

These three elements are the basis for the ideal of unity that
God so clearly wants; they are channels for the power necessary for truly Christian marriage. We can look on them as
three conversions: conversion to Christ, conversion to loving
the brethren, and conversion to the governmental order of
God's kingdom.

It is interesting in this light to look at the structure of the
letter to the Ephesians. The first three chapters talk about
our conversion to Christ and the sacrificial death of Jesus that
unites us with the Father. The next chapter and a half offers
instruction on the way we should act toward our brothers and
sisters in the Lord. And the last part of the letter talks about
the proper governmental order for such specific relationships
as the relationship of husband and wife.

What will each of these "conversions" mean practically?
How do they affect the unity of marriage? Let's look at the
three separately, to see what Scripture teaches us.

Conversion to Christ

Jesus is the source of all unity in the universe, including
the unity of husband and wife. Unless both partners have
taken Jesus as their Lord, they will not be able to achieve the
full unity that God desires for them. Why is this? How does
the Lordship of Jesus affect a couple's marriage?

For one thing, taking Jesus as one's Lord includes taking
him as a teacher. When both husband and wife take Jesus as
their teacher, he is able to train them together in the right
way of life. He will point out to them those habits and sins
they must repent of. He will mold them in one way of thinking and responding. As two disciples of the same master,
they will share a greater unity in their beliefs, their approach
to life, and their values.

If a husband and wife are not both taught by Jesus, they
often learn different approaches to life. Perhaps *The Ladies'
Home Journal* becomes her teacher, while *Sports Illustrated*

is his. As followers of such different teachers, they will find themselves in conflict more often than in unity.

Jesus also gives his disciples the gift of the Holy Spirit. Without the power of the Spirit, a husband and wife will not be able to make the personal changes needed for their growth into full unity. The Spirit is the one who can gradually change personalities, replacing the responses of the flesh with the responses of God's children. With his power, a couple can change the habits of fear or impatience or selfishness that damage their relationship. The extent of a couple's unity will depend on the extent to which they are opening their lives to the Holy Spirit, asking him to reveal their sins and lead them into the truth.

One of the main priorities for any Christian couple, then, is growth in their personal relationships with the Lord. They should support each other in having time each day for personal prayer, and take time together regularly for prayer. Another priority is Scripture study, which is an opportunity for both husband and wife to come to their teacher for more instruction.[1]

Coming to the Lord in prayer, seeking his word in Scripture, opening our lives to the action of his Spirit: these are the ways that a couple can turn to Jesus and let him build up their unity as husband and wife.

Living as brethren

Before two Christians become husband and wife, they are brother and sister in the Lord. Christian marriage is something that takes place between two of the Lord's disciples

---

1. Personal conversion to Christ is treated in much greater depth in my earlier book *Hungry for God: Practical Helps for Personal Prayer* (Doubleday, 1974; Spire, 1976). I recommend that book for readers who need to learn more about growing in prayer and in a relationship with God. For those who wish to begin regular Scripture reading, I recommend George Martin's *Reading Scripture as the Word of God* (Servant Books, 1975).

who have passed with him from death to life. Even after they marry, that remains their most fundamental relationship, and its strength will affect their unity as a couple. Unless they learn how to live as Christian brethren, they will have a hard time living as Christian husband and wife.

In my experience talking with married couples, I have found remarkably few marriage problems that really involve marriage itself. Some problems, sexual problems for example, are specifically related to marriage. But many, many more stem instead from a couple's failure to heed Scripture's teaching about how Christians should act toward their brothers and sisters. In fact, many of the most important Scripture passages for married Christians are not specifically directed to marriage at all, but deal with fundamental principles for living a Christian life.

Take the very common problem of resentment. Many persons with marriage problems harbor some kind of resentment against their partners. But Scripture's advice on dealing with resentment contains nothing specific to marriage. When the letter to the Ephesians says, "Do not let the sun go down on your anger" (4:26), it speaks to all Christians, married and single. All Christians are supposed to settle disagreements with their brothers and sisters quickly, before resentments develop.

Unfortunately, many Christians today never learn how to behave toward their brothers and sisters in the Lord. They simply follow whatever behavior the society around them considers acceptable, even though society and Scripture often disagree. In order to get this second basis for the unity of marriage firmly established, we need to go to Scripture to learn how to live as brethren. The best place to begin is with the most basic commandment of all: "Love one another as I have loved you" (John 15:12).

If we think about the way Jesus loved his disciples, we see that he got very little back from them. They constantly misunderstood or disappointed him; at times they even tried to obstruct his mission. Yet Jesus went right on loving them. His love never changed according to their response or lack of response; it always remained patient and steadfast.

Now Jesus tells us, his disciples, "I want you to love each other in the same way." He commands us to love our brothers and sisters no matter how they respond to us or treat us. Our love as Christians does not depend on the emotional support and rewards we receive in return. It is based on our decision to obey the commandment of Jesus. One way to explain this concept is to say that Christian love is based on commitment, not on feelings.

I sometimes wonder how many married Christians realize that their love as husband and wife is based on commitment, a covenant relationship, rather than feelings. I often hear people say that they are afraid that one day they will wake up and realize, "I don't love my partner anymore." What they mean is, "I am afraid that my feelings toward my partner will change—that I won't find him attractive, or that I won't feel close to her."

Feelings of attraction and closeness are, of course, important to marriage. A couple who feel distant or uninterested in each other have a problem, and in later chapters I will discuss some of the steps they can take to correct it. But that problem, significant as it is, need not call their basic love into question. Christian love, the love Jesus commands us to have toward our brothers and sisters (and so toward our husbands and wives), has nothing to do with two people feeling attracted or emotionally close. It is a love that remains faithful through good times and bad, for better or for worse.

Have you noticed how many couples today rewrite their marriage vows to eliminate those very words? Some of the new vows say explicitly, if more elegantly, "I promise to love as long as we're compatible." "I promise to love as long as this relationship helps me grow as a person." "I promise to love as long as you keep on your good behavior."

This trend in secular society highlights the uniqueness of

the commitments made in contracting a Christian marriage. A Christian husband and wife commit themselves to a love that fewer and fewer people in our world can or do promise. They enter a solemn life-long covenant that God stands behind.

I have seen marriages change completely once the partners understood that their love was not at the whim of their feelings, but rested on a decision they had made. One spouse might be getting all kinds of flack from the other. She might be turned off by his potbelly; he might be fed up with her nagging. But then they realize that those things do not determine their love. Instead they begin to look to God as the source of their love—God who can put his own love in our hearts as we decide to obey his commandment. Christian love is based on a decision and carried out with the help of the Holy Spirit, a power greater than our natural ability to love.

Jesus also tells us what this committed love means in practical terms of how we act toward our brothers and sisters. Through the writers of Scripture, he tells us how to live together and express our love. We learn that we should be ready to serve one another: "Have this mind among yourselves, which is yours in Christ Jesus, who, though he was in the form of God, did not count equality with God a thing to be grasped, but emptied himself, taking the form of a servant, being born in the likeness of men" (Phil. 2:5-7). We learn right attitudes to have toward one another: "Love one another with brotherly affection; outdo one another in showing honor" (Rom. 12:10). "Put on then, as God's chosen ones, holy and beloved, compassion, kindness, lowliness, meekness, and patience" (Col. 3:12). We learn practical things, like how to speak to each other: "Therefore, putting away falsehood, let everyone speak the truth with his neighbor, for we are members one of another" (Eph. 4:25). "Let all bitterness and wrath and anger and clamor and slander be put away from you, with all malice" (Eph. 4:31). "Teach and admonish one another in all wisdom" (Col. 3:16).

None of these instructions are addressed specifically to married Christians, yet all of them are vitally important for the relationship of husband and wife. Later on, when we talk about communication or about the specific roles of husband and wife, we will see these same principles applied. Yet at heart, they are not explicitly marriage principles, but general rules of conduct for all Christians.

Unfortunately, no Christian has reached the point where he will always and everywhere follow these rules of conduct perfectly. We act badly toward each other at times. We offend each other. Our weaknesses and failings show up. So Jesus gives us one more help for maintaining our love as brethren: he teaches us how to repair our wrongdoing and reconcile ourselves to one another.

In Matthew's gospel, Jesus tells us that whenever a Christian notices something wrong in his relationship with a brother or sister, he should take the initiative in resolving the problem. "If you are offering your gift at the altar, and there remember that your brother has something against you, leave your gift there before the altar and go; first be reconciled to your brother, and then come and offer your gift" (Matt. 5:23-24). Christian brethren should be eager to maintain their unity, eager to take any steps necessary to resolve their differences and restore the harmony of their relationship.

A person eager to maintain unity will also want to acknowledge failures quickly, without a big discussion of who is to blame. Don't try to analyze all the reasons why you yelled at your spouse: "30% tiredness, 30% my parents, 30% a bad childhood experience, and 10% me " Instead, own up to what you have done wrong, and make a straightforward request for forgiveness. "It was wrong for me to yell at you. I know I was tired, but that doesn't excuse me. I am sorry for hurting you, and I resolve not to do it again. Please forgive me."

Eagerness to maintain unity also means eagerness to forgive. Jesus tells us, "If your brother sins, rebuke him, and if he repents, forgive him; and if he sins against you seven times in the day, and turns to you seven times and says, 'I repent,' you must forgive him" (Luke 17:3-4). Don't try to judge the other person's motives; don't hold on to the incident so you can throw it in his face next time he fails. When your husband or wife repents, let your relationship be restored. Acknowledge that you know he or she is sorry for what happened, express your forgiveness, and let the incident be settled.[2]

Understanding the nature of Christian love, learning the right ways to act toward our brethren, maintaining love through repentance and forgiveness—the way of life that Jesus gave to all his disciples must also be followed by the Christian husband and wife.

Governmental Authority

As we usually see it exercised, authority seems to swing from one extreme to another. On the one hand, we see authority used as a means of oppression. So often in our world, authority is based on strength or power or wealth; those who wield it seem most interested in benefiting themselves at the expense of people who are poorer or weaker. To correct such oppression, many people suggest the opposite extreme—doing away with all authority, leaving everyone to do exactly as he pleases.

Neither extreme of authority can create and maintain unity in a group of people. A dictator can force people to work together, but he cannot unify them. All he can do is

---

2. The principles of repentance and forgiveness are of such importance that I urge any readers unfamiliar with them to find a full explanation. An excellent treatment can be found in talk eight of *Basic Christian Maturity*, a cassette tape course (Servant Cassettes, 1976).

create an efficient slave force. The total absence of authority does not create unity either, only chaos. People who do only what they please are rarely able to take united action.

God wants to establish authority in the social units that make up his kingdom precisely because he wants those groups to have unity and to take united action. The life of the Christian people contains a real element of authority and subordination—God does not want the chaos of everyone doing his own thing. But at the same time, the authority that marks God's kingdom is not to be of the oppressive or dominating kind we find in the world. It must be based on a completely different model.

The Lord offers us such a model in his own life in the Trinity. Through the Scriptures, especially the gospel of John, Jesus lets us glimpse the total equality shared by the persons of the Godhead. At the same time, he shows us a community life governed by a definite order. In his role as Son, Jesus always obeys the Father. During his life here on earth, Jesus never sought to fulfill himself or make a name for himself. He stated over and over again that his only desire was to obey his Father's commands. He yielded everything, even his life, to that. And as Jesus took the ultimate risk of submission, giving himself up to death on the cross, the Father raised him up in the glorious victory of the resurrection.

Jesus wants the life of his people to mirror this relationship between the Father and himself. When Scripture talks about receiving a new life from God or living the life of the Spirit, it is not talking about some internal, invisible activity confined to prayer. It is telling us to reproduce in our lives and our social structures the pattern of relationship we see in the Godhead.

Scripture tells us very clearly how we can follow that pattern within the family. For one thing, it says that parents have authority over their children. A mother and father are to govern the lives of their children, molding and training them to follow the Lord. Children, in turn, owe obedience and respect to their parents.

Scripture also establishes the husband's authority over his wife. The first letter to the Corinthians states: "The head of every man is Christ, the head of a woman is her husband, and the head of Christ is God" (11:3). In the letter to the Ephesians we read, "The husband is the head of the wife as Christ is the head of the church, his body" (5:23).

Today we often hear that Scripture's view of the husband's authority is simply a leftover from first century Jewish culture. Critics sometimes compare Paul's instructions on marriage to his instructions on slavery, an institution he accepted as part of his times, but which later generations of Christians condemned. In the same way, these critics argue, Paul accepted the idea of a husband's authority because it was part of his culture, but today we can freely reject it.

What this logic overlooks, however, is the difference between Paul's instructions to slaves and masters and his words to husbands and wives. Paul never stated that slavery ought to exist. He merely recognized the fact that some Christians of his day were slaves or slaveowners, and tried to point out how they should act as Christians in that situation.

But when Paul spoke to husbands and wives, he clearly intended to give more than a rule of conduct for particular cultural conditions. He saw his advice as having universal significance, for all times and all cultures, because he believed that it was based in a reality that transcends culture—the nature of God and the order of creation. In the passages I quoted above and in other scriptural instructions on marriage, we are told that the authority of the husband is directly linked to the unchanging reality of Christ's authority in the Church and the Father's authority in the life of the Trinity.

I also believe that the order of governmental authority in the family goes beyond cultural rules. I feel that we are touching here on something that is fundamental to God's plan for the unity of husband and wife. He wants to establish a seat of authority in marriage to focus and safeguard a couple's unity. Avoiding both the false unity of domination and the disunity of anarchy, he offers us the way that he himself takes—headship and submission in the Spirit of love.

The scriptural pattern for authority in the family carries no judgment on the value of either husband or wife. The wife's submission does not mean that she is passive, inferior, unequal, or immature, nor does the husband's authority say that he is better, smarter, or more important. There is an equality of worth between husband and wife in Christ, yet a distinction of responsibilities.

Authority and submission enable a husband and wife to move forward as one, just as Jesus' submission to his Father allowed God to act for our salvation. It does away with the struggle for power that paralyzes many marriages. It enables a couple to settle minor decisions quickly, saving their discussion time for more important matters. And it provides them with a way to settle their differences and move ahead when they cannot reach full agreement.

As a couple matures in Christ, they will find headship functioning more naturally, almost invisibly. Growing in unity of mind and heart, they will increasingly see things the same way, judge the same way, make decisions the same way. The tension of choosing his way or hers will diminish as they focus more and more on finding the Lord's way. But how headship should function at any given point in a couple's marriage will vary to some extent according to the degree of maturity they have reached. For this reason, while the fundamental principle of the husband's authority must be clearly expressed, there needs to be a certain flexibility in how headship operates.

Ordinarily, a couple will share responsibility for their family life. Both husband and wife will have particular spheres of responsibility in which they exercise authority. For example, if the wife knows how to manage the household or buy the children's clothes, it is appropriate for her husband to delegate these responsibilities to her. She can then take care of these duties without consulting her husband on every decision. In the same way, if the husband has shown that he can take care of the yard or the car, he should normally take on those responsibilities without always looking for input from his wife.

If the husband is more mature than his wife, both personally and as a Christian, he ought to take more responsibility for everything in their life together. As his wife demonstrates her ability and judgment he can then give over more authority and responsibility to her. His aim should be to help his wife learn and mature, so that she becomes capable of handling larger responsibilities.

If the wife is more mature, the husband should value and draw on his wife's wisdom and experience. At the same time, the wife should offer her advice in a way that supports her husband's ability to function as head of the family. If she simply takes over the leadership in subtle or obvious ways while waiting for him to mature, he will never learn how to fulfill his responsibilities. His exercise of headship can only mature when he actually functions as a head.

When decisions affecting the life of the whole family must be made, husband and wife should normally discuss the matter together thoroughly, looking for God's direction. Ordinarily, couples who discuss these decisions can reach an agreement on them. If they cannot, it is the husband's responsibility to decide how to settle the issue. He might exercise his authority by deciding to wait until the two of them can reach an agreement. He might decide to follow his wife's opinion, or to follow his own, or to seek outside counsel. The fact of his headship does not mean that a husband makes all the decisions by himself, or even that, in a conflict, his opinion must prevail. He seeks always to do what is wise and right.

In exploring these nuances of headship, I do not at all mean to minimize the husband's authority. As head, he exercises a real authority, which his wife should respect and obey. The wife's submission is not just a matter of her being favorably disposed to considering requests her husband makes. It involves real obedience. In fact, the true test of submission comes when a wife is faced with some decision of her husband's that she disagrees with. I am not referring here to a request that would break God's law or violate the wife's moral beliefs; no Christian need obey an order to sin. I am talking about decisions which are not sinful but which the wife happens to disagree with.

I remember one night several years ago when I asked my wife to put down something she was reading so that we could talk with the children. She kept reading. Later that evening, I pointed out to Anne that this was an example, although a trivial one, of unsubmissive behavior. As we discussed this, Anne admitted that she had been willing to submit to me only when she agreed with my requests or thought I was doing the right thing. We decided then to work toward the kind of submission that Scripture describes, in which Anne is ready to obey me even when she disagrees, simply because I am her husband.

One point which I should mention here is that headship and submission can best be learned when a couple see them at work in the larger Christian community. At the same time that Anne had to re-examine her feelings about submission, I was learning how to submit to another man who was my head in our Christian fellowship. I too was learning to obey even when I disagreed with a decision.

That was a great help for both of us; I could better understand what Anne was going through, and she could see me
working through the same problem she had to face.

Headship and submission can be a confusing idea. It is
not a formula solution to apply legalistically to marriage
problems. It is only one aspect of a much larger relationship. In later chapters, as I talk in more detail about the
specific roles of husbands and wives, I will present some
guidelines for the use of headship in the family, and give a
fuller picture of its exercise. The important thing to remember now is that headship is a gift from God to his
people. If we learn to exercise it in the wisdom and love of
the Holy Spirit, it can prove to be an important source of
unity and peace, enabling our marriages to reflect the
unity and love of Christ and the church.

God calls us as husband and wife to be perfectly one,
and he gives us the means to grow into that unity through
our relationship with him, our love for one another, and
the governmental order established for our well-being. To
take advantage of these means to unity, we must learn to
make them a practical part of our married life. One important step to doing this is to learn how to open up to one
another with our feelings, frustrations, and ideas. Free and
loving communication, the subject of the next chapter,
helps a couple discover how to overcome obstacles to their
unity in the Lord.

CHAPTER FOUR

COMMUNICATION

Having a successful Christian marriage does not mean that a husband and wife will never have any problems getting along with each other. All marriages run into problems and difficulties; that is a natural result of putting two people together to live a common life. But while every marriage includes its share of problems, one difference in a successful marriage is that husband and wife can get those problems resolved because they have developed regular, effective communication.

Lack of communication not only prevents a couple from dealing with their problems, it can actually create many problems in itself. I have talked to many couples whose marriages were in trouble. In most cases, the obvious grievances were not the real source of the trouble. The true problem was a lack of communication.

A few months before I began work on this book, a woman came to talk to me. She had grown up in a Christian home and had been married fifteen years to a Christian man. Yet she told me that she couldn't take it any longer—she was leaving her husband. He had not talked to her in four months; they had not had sexual relations for eight months. She didn't have any desire left for him; she didn't even want to see him again. She wanted out.

I asked if she had ever told her husband that she felt this way. She answered no.

I offered to try to help them if she would go home and tell her husband what she had told me. A week later they were both in my office to talk. During that conversation, the wife finally blurted out all the things bothering her. Her husband never did chores around the house; he never made repairs; he never talked to her; they never discussed the problems one of their three children was having; he always insulted her family. A whole range of problems possible in a marriage appeared.

I told the couple simply to talk together about their problems. We worked out several times when they could sit down each week to talk, and I told them to discuss the various problems one by one. We did agree on a simple program to ensure that the husband did the necessary chores—this had been a source of tremendous frustration for his wife—but on the whole I just urged them to establish a regular pattern of communication.

Within two months, that couple had changed. They were happy together. They were developing a satisfying sexual relationship. The teachers at school reported that the child who had been a problem was no longer fidgety and nervous. In two months, they had moved from complete desperation and had the makings of a strong, happy marriage. And it happened in large part because they had made regular communication a part of their life.

Communication will not transform every difficult marriage as dramatically as that. But this one story does show how important and effective it can be. And I am not talking about emergency, once-in-a-crisis communication, when problems get so bad that they force a couple to talk. I mean regular communication that goes on from day to day and week to week as part of the pattern of married life. A husband and wife who regularly talk freely and openly about their life together will find themselves facing fewer problems and dealing far more effectively with those that do arise.

Communication does more than solve problems. It also gives a couple the means to express and foster their love. It helps them grow in the unity of mind and heart that a Christian marriage should produce.

A husband and wife must be able to express their love for each other if that love is to have its full effect. Without communication, however, attempts to express love may fail. For example, a wife might try to show her love for her husband by inviting friends over for a party she thinks he will enjoy, when he would actually prefer to spend a quiet evening with her. Or a husband might try to show his love by giving his wife her favorite perfume on every birthday and anniversary, when she has enough perfume and would prefer another gift. Unless we stay in communication, we never know when expressions of love like these fall short. We must know each other—our needs, hopes, concerns—in order to express our love effectively.

In the same way, regular communication helps married couples grow in unity. The unity of a Christian marriage is based on our relationship with Christ, but it is normally realized and built up through communication. If we do not communicate about our individual relationships with the Lord, we will find it difficult to grow in a relationship to the Lord as couples. If we do not build a unity of mind and heart by discussing the various situations of our lives, we will not in fact be of one mind and heart. Regular communication in itself serves as a way of seeking that unity "which has the Spirit as its origin" (Eph. 4:3 NAB).

Everything I have said so far about the importance of communication is especially true for married couples today. We live in a time of such rapid social change that one day's agreements and solutions may not be adequate for the next day's problems. Jobs change, families move, the latest fad hits the teenagers—a couple needs good communication simply to keep pace with the changing circumstances of their life. They need a pattern of communication that guarantees them regular, frequent time to talk.

How can the average Christian couple develop such a pattern of communication?

They can start by taking two important steps. First, husband and wife must agree together on the importance of communication and decide to make it a high priority for their time and attention. Second, they must adopt some practical method to ensure that regular communication does take place. That usually means scheduling regular times together into their weekly routine.

Making Communication a Priority

Most couples will at least give lip service to the importance of communication, but their actual behavior often tells a different story. Many couples always seem ready to push aside their time together in order to make more room for the office, the bridge party, the children—even the prayer meeting. They treat communication as the very lowest item on their list of priorities.

Some couples do this because they honestly do not realize that they should take time to communicate. Others know that they need time together, but cannot bring themselves to say no to other demands in order to make room for it. If they are dedicated Christians, they may even feel guilty about saving time for themselves in the face of their other responsibilities.

My wife and I are grateful that the Lord taught us about the importance of communication even before we were married. One afternoon a few months before our wedding,

I was sitting on the floor of my apartment praying and sensed the Lord telling me that my future life would depend on the depth of my union with him and the depth of my union with Anne. Everything else in my life would flow from those two relationships: if they were not strong and continually deepening, nothing else I did would be fully fruitful.

I learned early on that to keep my relationship with the Lord strong, I must take time every day to be alone with him in prayer. It is good to pray while I am driving, sitting at my desk, brushing my teeth, mowing the lawn. It is good to pray with other Christians, at prayer meetings and in liturgical celebrations. But it is important that I also go into my room every day, close the door, and spend time alone with God. When I restrict my time with the Lord to times of public prayer or to prayer on the run, I miss an important dimension of my relationship with him. There is a sense of the Lord's presence and a quality of union with him that simply cannot exist unless I regularly take time for personal prayer.

In the same way, the quality of my relationship with Anne depends on our taking regular time together for communication. We can talk at the dinner table with our children and guests; we can talk while we do dishes together or get the kids ready for bed. But something is missing in the sense of our union as husband and wife when we are not taking regular time to open our lives to one another and seek wisdom for our responsibilities.

Taking time together to talk is not selfish. Neither is it optional or unimportant. Everything else we do with our lives—raising our children, serving the Lord, helping other people—will be affected by the communication we establish as married couples. It deserves a very high priority in our lives, even when we have to give up some favorite hobby, or turn down a chance to earn more money, or

cut back on service to our church or prayer group, in order
to create enough time for each other.

Scheduling Time Together

Once a couple determines to take time for communication, they must take some active steps to implement their
decision. That usually means scheduling regular times
during the week when they can talk.

I know that some people consider "schedule" a dirty
word. They think it means all restriction and no spontaneity. I will only say that if a couple can establish adequate,
regular time for communication without a schedule, they
do not need one. I have seen very few such couples. Most
couples I know never managed to find enough time for
communication until they began to schedule it in.

A schedule is a tool which helps us assert control over
the circumstances of our lives, instead of letting those circumstances control us. When we do not have a schedule,
we tend to treat competing demands for time and attention
on a first-come, first-served basis, rather than on the basis
of their relative importance. And so the children and the
relatives, the telephone and doorbell and television, all start
to crowd out the time we should devote to communication.

A schedule gives us a basis for saying yes or no to conflicting demands. Suppose someone calls up to invite a
couple to a bridge party on Monday night. If that time is
not scheduled for communication, they will probably accept without even considering whether they should spend
that evening talking. But if they had that Monday night
reserved for each other, they could say, "No. We already
have plans for that evening." A husband who is asked to
discuss business over lunch will not be likely to turn down
the invitation so that he can spontaneously take his wife
out for lunch. But if he and his wife have agreed to have
lunch together on that day, he can say, "Sorry, I have

another appointment." Scheduling helps us implement our basic decision to give communication a high priority.

When it comes to setting up scheduled times together, the pattern of each couple's life will vary. One question is, how much time does a couple need for communication? For most marriages, I believe that husband and wife should take at least two to five hours a week specifically to talk to each other. Some couples may want to take this all at one time once a week; others may prefer to have several hour or half-hour sessions. A couple who are still establishing basic communication may need more time; other couples, who have good communication already, may need less. But virtually all couples at all times in their relationships need to take some regular time together to communicate about their relationship and common responsibilities.

Again, this should be time in addition to the regular flow of daily conversation. Ordinary conversation is very important in itself, but it cannot substitute for time to discuss important matters seriously and at length.

Where do a husband and wife find this time to spend together? The differing circumstances of each couple's life make it impossible to give blanket rules, but I can mention some times that other couples have used successfully. Couples who have no children, or whose children have grown and left home, often find adequate time for good communication during meals. Couples with children usually have more difficulty, as they need to find times when they can be alone.

Lunchtime is one possibility. Some husbands work close enough to home to stop in for lunch several times a week while the children are at school. Some couples can arrange to meet for lunch near the husband's place of work, or near the wife's if she works outside the home.

Other couples may find the evening a better time to spend together. I know one family with six children in which the parents sit down to talk after dinner, while the older children do dishes and help the younger ones get ready for bed. Many couples are able to take one evening a week as an opportunity to talk in depth, either going out or staying at home. Some are able to get together several nights a week after putting the children to bed.

Couples who are very busy may find that even these times will not work. But I have never met any couple, no matter how busy, who could not find some regular time to spend together once they agreed to make communication a high priority and started looking for the time with determination. It may take some ingenuity, but we *can* find the time.

Once a couple has established some special time for communication, they should take care to protect it from interruption. If other activities come up for the evenings they have agreed to spend together, they should normally say no. We would not lightly break an appointment with an important business associate or with the mayor of the city, and we should not lightly break appointments with our partners in life. If changing circumstances disrupt an established schedule for communication—say the Cub Scouts meeting changes from Wednesday to Thursday, or lunch time at the office changes, or a favorite inexpensive restaurant closes—we should grab the first available time to sit down together and work out a new schedule, not letting these changes discourage us or destroy our practice of communication. Protecting time for good communication is no indulgence; it is essential to the strength of a marriage.

What Do We Talk About?

After a couple agrees to make communication a priority and schedules regular times to spend together, they have one step left to take. They have to sit down and start talking. And when a husband and wife who have not been communicating sit down for the first time specifically to talk, they can feel very awkward. It is not unusual for one or both partners to go completely blank and have nothing to talk about. Afterward the husband may complain that he didn't know what to say, or the wife may feel that they didn't talk about anything important.

To some degree, this initial awkwardness is unavoidable. The channels of communication that have grown stiff with disuse simply need some time to grow supple again. But it does help for both husband and wife to have some idea, and the same idea, about what they should discuss. At the risk of sounding too elementary, I would like to list some topics that a couple should talk about when they get together.

One important subject for communication is each partner's daily life. I am often amazed to discover how many husbands and wives have only the vaguest idea of what their partners do during all the hours of the day they spend apart. This lack of knowledge makes it harder to understand, support, and strengthen one another.

To stay in touch with one another's daily life, we need to talk about the people and responsibilities that we each face from day to day. Whom do we deal with in our daily and weekly routines? Do we have good relationships with these people? Do we need wisdom or encouragement for some problem in a particular relationship? What are our major responsibilities during the day? Are we succeeding with them? Where do we need wisdom or strength in facing them?

Husbands and wives also need to talk regularly about the relationships and responsibilities that make up their common life. When a man and woman marry, they give up two independent, unrelated lives to put all their resources and responsibilities together. A married couple does not need to join a monastery to experience total Christian community: they already live (or should be living) a totally committed, all-embracing communal life by virtue of their marriage. The family is a covenanted Christian community, a little church in itself.

As the pastoral leaders of this community, husband and wife must regularly discuss all aspects of its life so they can reach agreements on how to handle them. They need to talk about the children, finances, schedules, in-laws, vacations—everything that makes up their life together.

Finally, a couple should communicate about their individual relationships with the Lord. They should talk about their daily prayer times, the lessons they learn in prayer and any problems they encounter. They should share insights received while reading Scripture. They should discuss together what they believe God is doing in their church or prayer group, and the ways they can respond as individuals and as a family.

If a husband and wife do not discuss these aspects of their individual relationships with Christ, they will not develop the full unity they should have in their common relationship with him. This can be especially true today, when many couples are experiencing newly awakened or deepened Christian lives in a time of great spiritual renewal. These couples need good communication in order to grow together in the fuller Christian life opening before them.

From the suggestions above it should be clear that I am not recommending that husbands and wives communicate purely for the sake of communication. I am talking about an essentially practical kind of communication, designed to strengthen a couple's life together. "Communication" has acquired such mystique of late that I hesitated even to use the word in this chapter. I hear it discussed in terms of "self-fulfillment" or "self-exploration," terms that tend to minimize its practical function and place it instead in a context of self-concern and indulgence.

The pattern of communication I recommend is not primarily a means to "self-fulfillment." It is a means to ensure that the part of the body of Christ for which we are responsible—our marriages and families—can function well and become strong in the Lord. It calls not for a spirit of self-concern, but for self-sacrificial love and an eagerness for unity.

CHAPTER FIVE

OBSTACLES TO COMMUNICATION

The steps to regular communication outlined in the previous chapter will not automatically produce wonderful openness. Even when they sit down regularly to talk together, some couples find it difficult to open up and share the feelings and concerns they know they should discuss. Any number of problems can lie behind these blocks in communication. In this chapter, I want to discuss some of the most common of these problems.

Attitudes That Block Communication

Many breakdowns in communication stem from bad attitudes about ourselves, our partners, or even about communication itself. For example, some husbands and wives maintain very rigid attitudes about the division of responsibilities in the family. A wife may feel that the way she runs the house or spends her time during the day is none of her husband's business. A husband may feel that his duty to the family stops with his paycheck, and that his wife should raise the children and worry about the in-laws. Naturally, when these attitudes prevail, neither partner is able to express interest in the other's responsibilities or receive advice about his own.

It is right that each partner in a mature marriage have

certain spheres of authority and responsibility, but the couple should not seal these areas off from each other behind rigid barriers. To do so is to seal off the insights, wisdom, love, and support that one partner can give the other. It represents a retreat from the spirit and practice of community life that a husband and wife have covenanted themselves to live. It may also represent a husband's refusal to accept his responsibility to care for the whole life of the family as head of the marriage, or a wife's refusal to accept the pastoral direction and care of her husband.

Another attitude that blocks communication seems to appear most commonly in men. Some husbands consider themselves incommunicative by nature and feel it is unreasonable for their wives to expect them to talk. Many men actually do have trouble communicating, but they cannot simply decide, "This is how I am. Adjust to it." They must realize that a failure to communicate often means a failure to love; it is a serious weakness that can destroy a marriage. Incommunicative husbands should resolve to open up and talk. God wants them to change and will help them do so.

Sometimes, however, a husband's incommunicativeness can be aggravated by what seems to him an inordinate curiosity on his wife's part. While silent husbands should learn to open up, their wives must also realize that they do not need to discuss every conceivable topic with their husbands. He does not need to know every detail of the neighbors' new color scheme, and she does not need to hear every bit of news from his office. If a husband who already tends to be incommunicative gets a barrage of unnecessary or prying questions from his wife, he usually retreats even further into silence. This in turn may goad his wife into more determined efforts to draw him out, starting a vicious cycle that causes frustration and dissatisfaction on both sides.

Once a couple gets entrenched in such a cycle, they may

have a very hard time pulling out. One couple who came to talk to me about their marriage had let a pattern of non-communication build up for years, until the frustrations it caused actually began to threaten their emotional health. Virtually anytime the wife tried to communicate with her husband, she expressed so much anger and frustration that I could easily understand her husband's incommunicativeness. Yet I could also see that her husband used his wife's anger to excuse his own failure to communicate.

The changes that had to take place in their marriage were very slow and painful, unlike the rapid transformation of the couple I mentioned in another chapter. Their reactions to one another were so deeply embedded that they would go weeks at a time without making any visible progress toward overcoming them. It was painful for the husband to accept that he needed to change, that failure to communicate was a failure to love. It was difficult for the wife to be patient and trust that her husband could change or even wanted to. After a year of struggling with their problems, the change in their marriage was by no means complete. But at least both partners knew the direction in which they had to keep moving if their marriage was to become all that they and the Lord wanted.

One help in breaking a cycle of noncommunication is greater sensitivity to the individual needs of each partner. A husband is not usually ready for a lot of information or questions the minute he steps in the door after a long day at work. At the same time, if his wife has spent a long day at home with the children, she will not want to spend an evening in silence. Simply recognizing each partner's situation goes a long way toward helping both adjust to these needs. A couple might agree that the husband can take his first half-hour home to relax, but then spend some time with his wife after dinner instead of immediately turning on the television or reading the newspaper.

Friendships with other Christians can also help break a

cycle of non-communication by relieving the pressure on the husband and wife's conversation. Rather than get frustrated because her husband will not talk about dress patterns, a woman should probably talk about them with other women who enjoy sewing. And if a husband finds his wife could care less about the World Series, he should probably save his sports-talk for some male friends who would join in. Establishing a sense of sisterhood among the women and brotherhood among the men in a Christian community provides a balance that can help the relationship between husband and wife.

One final attitude that can block communication is a reluctance to share burdens and problems appropriately with one's partner. Sometimes a husband may not be able to persuade his obviously upset wife to tell him what is bothering her. Or a wife may see that her husband is irritable, but get no response when she asks why.

Reluctance to open up to each other about our problems often reflects fear of burdening our partners, or even shame that we have problems. I have talked with many Christian wives who would not tell their husbands about particular needs or problems because they were afraid they would become a burden.

The reluctance may also have its roots in past frustrations. Perhaps previous experience has convinced a husband that his wife does not understand his problems, and cannot help him even if he shares them. Or a wife may remember some time when her husband shrugged off her problems as if they didn't exist.

Obviously, more is involved here than a simple refusal to communicate. But we should always bear in mind that normally a refusal to communicate seals off any possibility of solving the problem. To refuse to communicate is often to refuse to hope or love or forgive. Almost never is it a permissable stance for Christian husbands and wives.

Patterns of Speech That Block Communication

We can create many obstacles to successful communication simply by the way we talk to each other. If a husband regularly speaks harshly or critically to his wife, she will be understandably reluctant to open up to him. Failing to listen to a partner, regularly interrupting him, or finishing her sentences are other patterns of speech that create serious obstacles to good communication. Yet many people are surprisingly careless about the ways they speak to their marriage partners.

The attitude that often lies behind this carelessness is a feeling that people should be able to act any way they want within their families. We tend to view the home as a place to "be ourselves," meaning that we need not be concerned about how we talk to or treat our partners and children. Some people even prize very free behavior in the home as a sign of honesty.

Honesty in communication is important, but it is also important to recognize that the Lord wants us to take responsibility for the way we talk to others and express our feelings. Harsh, unloving ways of speaking are sinful, whether in our homes or outside them, because they violate our Christian commitment to treat other people with love and respect. We need to recognize when we speak unlovingly to our marriage partners and resolve to change with their help and the help of God.

Often, we ourselves may be blind to some pattern of harsh speech. Here husbands and wives need to help each other. We should learn how to point out lovingly to our partners those patterns of speech which disturb us, and we should be willing to listen to what they tell us about the way we talk to them. At one point in my own marriage, I realized that I often spoke impatiently to Anne. I began to ask her forgiveness each time this happened. One day,

Anne said that she could not keep forgiving me if I did not try to change the way I talked to her. That really helped me. I was forced to realize that I had taken my impatience too lightly and had not made any serious, sustained effort to change.

I began to take my impatience to the Lord in prayer, asking him to help me overcome it. One day as I prayed about the problem, I felt that God wanted me to understand that impatience *never* helps. It never resolves a situation; it only adds another obstacle to communication. I took "impatience never helps" as my slogan, and from that day I saw a gradual but definite change in the way I talked to Anne. The same kind of change can happen to anyone who decides to face unloving patterns of speech for what they are and root them out.

Unfortunately, many husbands and wives take the wrong approach when they try to correct their partners' speech. Often their own worst patterns of speech surface and turn the whole discussion into a fight. Suppose a wife decides that she must speak to her husband about the way he interrupts her. If she bursts out, "You hate me, and that's why you always interrupt," she is not going to get a reasonable response. He will probably snap back, "Oh, you're always nagging me," thus starting a bitter argument. A few rounds like that can discourage anyone from trying to correct a partner.

We all need to learn to accept correction without reacting defensively, but we must also learn how to correct each other without sounding harsh or accusatory. We should never question our partners' basic love and commitment to us, condemn them, speculate about their motives, or make absolute judgments. Rather than say, "You always criticize me in front of our friends," we should try to state our feelings objectively and without accusations. For instance, "When Bill and Mary were over last night, I felt embarrassed by what you said about my cooking. I feel this has happened a lot lately. Are you being too critical, or am I over-sensitive?"

By refraining from absolute statements and accusations, we help our partners listen to us without defensiveness. By admitting that our own perception of the problem may be wrong, or at least incomplete, we help our partners admit that they might also be wrong.

In order to make corrections helpfully, we may need to wait for the right time to bring a matter up. We might want to wait for an incident that provides a good example of the behavior that bothers us. If we are very upset, we may need to wait until we are calm enough to discuss the matter without heated feelings.

If we wait, however, we should be careful not to wait too long. When we let problems build up, we usually end by dumping everything on our partners at once, with an additional load of high-pressure feelings. We need wisdom and sensitivity, gained through both experience and the guidance of the Spirit, in order to improve our communication.

If a discussion on a sensitive issue does get off track and feelings start rising, someone has to step in and stop it. Otherwise the discussion may escalate into more and more extreme charges. For example, a husband complains that the toast is burnt. His wife responds, "Well, you spilled paint on the garage floor." He comes back, "That was only once. You haven't cooked a decent breakfast in years." "If you ever did anything right around the house, I'd feel more like cooking a decent breakfast." And on and on they go.

If a conversation takes this course, either husband or wife should break it off and suggest returning to the original topic another time. Sometimes a suggestion to turn to the Lord and pray together can help establish a climate for reasonable discussion. But such suggestions should not be stated in a way that blames the other person for the argument. That is, we should not say, "*You* are obviously not able to talk calmly about this right now, so let's wait till tomorrow." A better way to break the discussion would be, "Okay, we don't seem to be getting anywhere. Why don't we stop and talk about this later?"

With a little experience, husbands and wives may even learn to recognize times and circumstances which make for tense discussions. One couple I know had moved to a new city and found that driving around town could trigger a lot of tensions. He would drive, she would read the map, and he always became impatient when she could not give him directions in time for him to act on them. I suggested that they discuss this problem sometime when they were not actually driving and reach some realistic agreement about what they could expect of each other when they were in the car.

Anne and I have learned to avoid difficult subjects late at night, when we are both too tired to be fully rational. We have also learned that if one of us feels particularly tired or pressured, the other should wait for a better time before offering a correction. Other couples will discover the particular situations in which they are especially prone to tension. Usually a little patient communication will help them learn how to handle them.

Fears that Block Communication

One last area that can create problems in communication is fear. Many husbands and wives are simply afraid to discuss certain difficulties or feelings with their partners. I've talked to individuals who carried some burden alone for years because they were afraid to talk about it. They were afraid to talk about their dislike for the in-laws or afraid to tell what they were experiencing or not experiencing sexually. They were afraid to bring up some concern about the children or to mention those little habits of their partners' that were so irritating.

The root of these fears is often concern about hurting the other person. Or a person may be afraid that once the problem appears in the open, it will prove to have no solution, and the total situation will be worse than before. Sometimes a husband or wife is afraid of being selfish—"It would be selfish for me to bring up this problem, because I would only be trying to make things better for myself." Some Christians overspiritualize their problems, feeling that they should bear the difficulty in silence because that would be sacrificial.

Forbearance certainly has a place in Christian marriage, but normally the Lord wants us to discuss our problems, even those problems we are afraid to discuss. We *can* work them out. Our partners are usually able to accept and handle far more than we think, and the Lord will help us when we face a problem that does go beyond our resources.

In fact, it will be good for both our partners and ourselves to face problems openly and deal with them. We will mature, and our marriages will mature. Our relationships will become more genuine and adult because we have had to face difficult problems as couples and work them through.

Where Do We Begin?

How do you begin putting all these principles for good communication into action for your marriage? You can make an excellent start by talking with your partner about this book. If you are reading the book together, you can decide to establish time for regular communication, following the guidelines outlined here. And you can use that time to discuss the other advice given in this book: about sex, raising children, being a husband or a wife, growing in unity and love, and so on.

Many people, however, will not be reading this book with their spouses. Perhaps your husband or wife is too busy to read the book now, or does not want to read it now, or doesn't even want to talk about marriage and family life now. It is very important that you be sensitive to his or her feelings and ask God for wisdom about how to communicate about this book.

Your partner may respond to a suggestion that he or she would find the book interesting. Then again, your partner might violently object to such a suggestion. You may be able to get across in a low-key, non-accusatory way some of the information here that would help your marriage or family. Whatever your situation, please do not use this book as ammunition for your ideas about marriage. You would do better to focus on those suggestions in the book that can help you better love and serve your partner and children, rather than on those ideas which would help your partner love and serve you. If this book does help you become more loving and supportive of your family, your partner is more likely to want to read it.

In the book of Sirach, we read that three things are delightful to the Lord and to men: "agreement between brothers, friendship between neighbors, and a wife and husband who live in harmony" (25:1). Regular communication is an important element in establishing that harmony between wife and husband. Our effort to establish communication will be well rewarded as it contributes to the peace and unity God desires for our marriages.

As a couple gets accustomed to talking regularly and freely, they find it easier to discuss sensitive areas of their life, such as their sexual relationship. Husbands and wives are often unaware of each other's basic attitudes toward sex, nor are they sure what attitudes are right for Christians to hold. In the next chapter, I will discuss a basic Christian view of sex.

CHAPTER SIX

THE CHRISTIAN VIEW OF SEX

During the 1960's, a great to-do was made in many Western countries about the "sexual revolution." A number of psychologists and sex researchers were urging people to shed their "Victorian repressions" and experiment with new, supposedly more exciting, sexual experiences. Some of the more extreme ideas of the sexual revolution gradually faded from the scene; one doesn't hear a great deal any more about group marriages or swinger's parties. But as a movement, this revolution was very successful in persuading our society to accept almost any form of sexual behavior.

Today, it is hard to pick up any magazine, turn on the television, go to a movie, or even walk down the street without encountering some sort of sexual suggestion. And those who are unwilling to cast aside all morality as a Victorian repression now find themselves accused of bigotry.

To live in such a society and retain their moral bearings, modern Christians need to be especially well grounded in the Christian view of the meaning and purpose of sex. Unfortunately, at the very time that need has become most urgent, the churches seem unable to give us clear direction. Theologians, spiritual writers, ministers and scripture scholars, in a hurry to shed their repressions, have sometimes lost a distinctively Christian moral view. Even when official church leaders do speak out clearly to defend traditional teaching, a chorus of dissenting voices manages to drown out, or at least confuse, their message.

Concerned Christians must face the fact that today they can no longer trust everything said about sex in a Christian magazine or from a pulpit. There is simply too much confusion within the churches on fundamental issues. What we must do is come directly to grips with the scriptural teaching about our sexuality, as that teaching has been preserved by generations of Christians and as it is being faithfully taught today in some Christian churches.

This is not to say that we should simply jump back to a nineteenth century Christian understanding of sex. Some older Christian teaching *has* carried an overlay of negative and repressive attitudes. But the solid core of basic scriptural teaching remains the norm by which we ought to judge all other opinions.

What I intend to do in this chapter is to present a basic Christian understanding of sex, based upon Scripture and the usual teaching of the churches. We can then see how this view contrasts with the understanding of sex that our society offers us, and examine its implications for Christian marriage. In the next chapter, I will discuss some of the practical steps a married couple can take to build a healthy, loving sexual relationship.

What Does Scripture Say?

The most obvious truth that Scripture teaches about sex is that it is part of God's design for human life: "Male and female he created them" (Gen. 1:27). Sexuality was not an accident or result of sin; it is an essential part of our divinely created nature.

The fact that sex comes from God tells us at once of its basic goodness. Sexuality in its broad sense, as an integral part of each person's identity and being, is obviously good. But the more specifically genital aspects of sex are equally good. The physical attraction we feel toward the opposite sex, our desires for sexual union, the pleasure received in intercourse—all this is part of our sexual nature as God created it.

As one of God's gifts, however, sex is not ours to use in any way we please. God has a purpose behind his creation and wants us, as responsible stewards, to respect his purpose in the way we use his gifts.

Part of the created purpose of our sexual faculties is the conception and birth of children. Our very bodies reveal God's intention in this regard: the whole biological purpose of intercourse is to bring sperm and ovum together so that a new life can begin. In Genesis, God tells the newly created man and woman, "Be fruitful and multiply" (1:28). His gift of sex is inextricably bound up with the creation of new life.

Scripture expressly condemns sexual practices like homosexuality and bestiality, which negate the procreative purpose of sex. Not that every act of intercourse must be intended to result in conception, but when we use our sexual organs, we should respect their reproductive design. That is why traditional Christian teaching maintains that heterosexual, genital intercourse is the proper form for physical sexual expression.

Procreation is not the only purpose of sexual intercourse. We also learn from Scripture that the Lord designed our sexuality as a key element in his plan to make husband and wife truly one flesh. Intercourse expresses in vivid physical terms the self-surrender, profound intimacy and total union that belong to the marriage covenant. It is this act above all that establishes the bond of unity between husband and wife. Most civil and religious authorities will not even recognize a marriage until it has been sexually consummated.

Because intercourse has such serious spiritual implications, Christian teaching has always asserted that it should take place only within the framework of life-long, committed marriage. Paul argues against sexual immorality on the grounds that "He who joins himself to a prostitute becomes one body with her" (1 Cor. 6:16). In other words, the sexual act in itself establishes a bond that God intended as serious and permanent. Intercourse outside the marriage covenant represents a denial of God's intention.

Scripture insists on the sexual fidelity of marriage partners; the Old Testament ranks adultery with murder as the most serious of sins. Substantial practical reasons can be given for married fidelity: it is important to the stability of the family unit, to the happiness of marriage partners and their children. Yet Scripture emphasizes fidelity not only for these reasons, but also because of the important spiritual dimensions of the act of intercourse.

As we look further into the meaning and purpose of the sexual relationship, we find that it embodies in a special way the covenant between Christ and his church that is the pattern for Christian marriage. The unbroken fidelity of husband and wife, the intimacy and the depth of their union, the denial of self to serve the other—these stand as visible signs of what Christ wants to establish in his relationship with his people.

What Does Our Culture Say?

Many Christians have formed their personal attitudes toward sex less on the basis of Scripture than on ideas current in the secular society around us. Depending on individual circumstances of where we grew up and how we were taught, we may have picked up attitudes ranging from extreme prudishness to complete amorality. Once we understand our sexuality in Christian terms, we need to re-evaluate those attitudes we have already formed. If necessary, we should be willing to change our way of thinking to make it conform to God's word.

The most problematic attitudes that our culture imparts fall into two categories—negative attitudes that create guilt or fear about sex, and hedonistic attitudes that exalt sexual pleasure to an importance beyond its created purpose. One or the other of these opposite tendencies has often prevailed in Western culture, but both of them fall short when judged against Scripture.

Negative Attitudes

Christianity is often blamed for the guilt and repressiveness that permeate some of our cultural attitudes toward sex. The blame is not completely misdirected; Christians *have* played a part in passing down these negative attitudes. Some Christian teaching on sexuality has placed all its emphasis on sexual control, paying scant attention to the basic goodness of our sexuality and of sexual expression in marriage.

Most churches are now trying to correct such imbalances, but the earlier teaching has already had its effect on many Christians. They have been left with guilty, fearful, or uneasy attitudes toward sex. Now they find it hard to respond freely and joyfully in sexual relations with their marriage partners.

Yet while Christians have had a part in handing down negative attitudes toward sex, we should not be fooled into thinking that these attitudes were ever part of the true scriptural picture. Repressive attitudes crept into Christian teaching not from the Bible or authentic tradition, but from various non-Christian philosophies. For example, a third-century Christian sect called Manichaeism picked up a pagan philosophical belief in the total corruption of the body. Believing the body to be inherently evil, they naturally considered physical sexual expression evil.

Other Christians recognized and condemned the error

of Manichaeism, but it managed to have some influence on orthodox Christian teachers. Some of the negative attitudes toward sex that have persisted among Christians can ultimately be traced back to the Manichaean influence. But this diluted pagan philosophy clearly has nothing to do with the truth we find in God's Word.

As we have already seen, Scripture teaches very clearly that our sexuality is intrinsically good. God made us sexual beings; he designed our sexual impulses and desires; he wanted us to be able to experience physical pleasure in intercourse. It is only when we misuse God's creation, exploiting our sexual faculties while ignoring their created purpose, that we sin.

Christians who have a problem with negative feelings about sex usually need to get straight on the fact that sexuality is truly good. After all, God could have designed a completely different way for the human race to increase and multiply. Sex is the way he chose; he wants husband and wife to enjoy his gift of sexual love.

These Christians may also find it helpful to remove any confusion about the difference between desire and lust, temptation and sin. I have talked with women who believed that any active desire for intercourse with their husbands amounted to lust, and to men who thought themselves sinful or perverted because they experienced sexual temptations. Understanding that desire is not lust nor temptation sin helped these people overcome their unfounded guilt.

Sexual desire is an eagerness for physical sexual union with another person. Far from being wrong, that desire is a very good and wholesome thing. It only becomes a problem when it gets out of control, beginning to dominate us. Uncontrolled desires will fix on an inappropriate object—say a man or woman other than our marriage partner—and cause an obsession with that person. Or they might fix on some inappropriate type of sexual behavior—perhaps reading pornography—and cause us to be obsessed with that. Whatever form the domination takes, it is something very different from the natural, healthy desire God created. It is this domination that we call lust.

A similar distinction separates temptation and sin. Temptation is an urge to do something wrong, either to commit a wrong action or neglect a good one. Sexual temptations are very common; almost all people experience at least an occasional temptation to some kind of sexual sin. But temptation only becomes a sin when we act on it—when we actually give in to lust or commit some wrong act. Even when a sexual temptation has caused us to feel some degree of pleaure, we have not sinned unless we have actually welcomed the tempting thought—received it and dwelt on it and let it take hold of us. Temptation is not sin; acting on temptation is.

Those of us who have a hard time recognizing the basic goodness of our sexuality or distinguishing between desire and lust, temptation and sin, should bring this problem to the Lord. We can ask him to bring to the surface any fears, past experiences, or old ideas that contribute to the guilt and fear we feel. The Lord and his Spirit can then begin to lead us to the truth. God wants to heal and free his people in this as in every part of their lives.

It is also good to be open about these problems with our marriage partners, asking for their support to work toward a better attitude. We may even want to discuss the matter with a trustworthy Christian brother or sister who is in a position to offer counsel. By taking some steps like these in the right direction, we will eventually see real improvement.

Pagan Attitudes

Any blocks and inhibitions that prevent Christians from enjoying a healthy sexual relationship in marriage can and should be overcome. At the same time, however, we should be wary of picking up the hedonistic attitude that marks so much of our culture. Many people today seek sexual gratification for its own sake. In their eyes, anything that gives sexual pleasure is automatically good.

That attitude has spread rapidly throughout our society. Sometimes we will find it blatantly argued, sometimes only subtly suggested. It is an attitude that Christians must be especially careful to resist, not only because it completely disregards God's Word about the purpose of sex, but because it pushes God himself aside to exalt sexual pleasure in his place. When people focus their entire lives on a search for sexual gratification, we have to conclude that they have made it a god.

In the letter to the Romans, Paul indicates a direct link between rejection of God and a life ruled by lust:

> ... although they knew God they did not honor him as God or give thanks to him, but they became futile in their thinking and their senseless minds were darkened ... Therefore God gave them up in the lusts of their hearts to impurity, to the dishonoring of their bodies among themselves, because they exchanged the truth about God for a lie and worshiped and served the creature rather than the Creator, who is blessed forever.
>
> (Rom. 1:21-25)

That is really happening in our society. As genuine belief in God wanes, more and more people turn to sex to find purpose for their lives. The ancient Greeks and Romans had their gods and goddesses of sex; now enlightened modern man is creating his.

Almost anything that we read or hear about sex today is liable to reflect a basically idolatrous attitude. In my research for this book, I noticed a disturbing cycle in the many books and manuals that discuss how to improve one's sex life. Most of these books place an enormous emphasis on the intensity and novelty of a couple's sexual experiences, subtly shifting the central focus of marriage onto purely sexual dimensions. And since the authors can only say so much about the mechanics of sex and only suggest so many positions for intercourse, they tend to take their search for sexual pleasure into a whole realm of practices—like sado-masochism, bi-sexuality, oral and anal intercourse—that pervert God's purpose for our sexual faculties.

This was the route taken a few years ago by two very popular manuals. I reviewed the first when it appeared, and found a great deal of material that would be helpful for Christian couples. But I also noticed a tone and spirit in the book, more marked in some sections than others, that revealed an underlying attitude incompatible with Christian views. The sequel, which appeared a couple of years later, confirmed my suspicions. The book encouraged people to try such "techniques" as group sex, bi-sexuality, and masturbation as means of improving their sex lives.

Some Christian authors have fallen into the same trap. About ten years ago, a Roman Catholic couple published an excellent book about the sexual relationship of married couples. It combined sound physiological advice with a thoroughly Christian point of view. But the authors' later books were preoccupied with telling couples how to achieve the most intense sexual pleasure possible. Gradually, the attitude underlying their work has slipped away from Christian principles and practice. The same could be said of many recent books on sex from both Protestant and Catholic sources.

Even supposedly objective scientific surveys of human sexual behavior tend to push their readers toward particular practices or beliefs. A survey by its nature carries a certain weight in influencing values: when we see that a large percentage of the population accepts certain ideas, those ideas seem more reasonable. Some of the recent sex surveys were actually sponsored by groups interested in promoting particular sexual attitudes, attitudes opposed to Christian beliefs. My point here is not to dispute the findings of these reports, although their scientific basis is often shaky, but to emphasize that literally any information on sex that our society offers may be colored by a pagan ideology.

Meanwhile, evidence is coming in about the effect that overemphasis on sexual gratification can have on marriage. Edward Shorter, a historian of the family, observes:

> ... the intensification of the couple's erotic life that we discussed above has injected a huge chunk of high explosive into their relationship. Because sexual attachment is notoriously unstable, couples resting atop such a base may easily be blown apart. To the extent that erotic gratification is becoming a major element in the couple's collective existence, the risk of marital dissolution increases."[1]

It appears that a scriptural attitude toward the place of sex in marriage offers purely practical advantages for a couple's stability and happiness that pagan attitudes cannot match.

Christian Attitudes in Sexual Relations

The difference between scriptural attitudes toward sex and one or the other cultural attitude are not purely philosophical. Our attitudes will determine a great deal about what actually happens in the sexual relationship we build with our partners. If we cling to negative attitudes, our sexual relations will be ridden with guilt and fear. If

---

1. Shorter, *The Making of the Modern Family* (Basic Books, 1975), p. 278.

we adopt a hedonistic attitude, we will be trusting our relationship to the "high explosive" of sexual attraction.

But what will happen if we hold fast to scriptural Christian attitudes? What kind of sexual relationship will we develop?

I will discuss here four qualities that characterize sexual relations patterned on truly Christian norms. This will not cover every attribute of sex in a Christian marriage. I simply want to present some of the most important implications that a scriptural attitude toward sex has for a couple's relationship.

Joyful

From all that I have said about the basic goodness of sex, it should already be clear that a Christian husband and wife can feel genuine freedom and joy in their sexual relations. God designed sexual intercourse as a source of great pleasure; we can be sure that he delights in seeing married couples enjoying this gift of his. We should approach our sexual relations in marriage with a real spirit of enjoyment. This is a time when we can relax and find pleasure in each other.

As Christians, we don't have to be bound by guilt or fear in our sexual relations. Nor do we have to live up to some exaggerated pagan standard for sexual performance. Under the lordship of Christ and the power of the Holy Spirit, we can experience the joy and freedom of marriage as God created it.

Committed

We usually think of sexual commitment in marriage only in terms of the fidelity of husband and wife. Certainly, that is a critically important aspect of commitment in marriage. But the concept of commitment also has implications for the way a couple conducts their sexual relationship. The most explicit instructions that Scripture offers for sexual relations in marriage tell us that husband and wife are committed to be available to one another sexually:

> The husband should give to his wife her conjugal rights, and likewise the wife to her husband. For the wife does not rule over her own body, but the husband does; likewise, the husband does not rule over his own body, but the wife does. Do not refuse one another except perhaps by agreement for a season, that you may devote yourselves to prayer; but then come together again, lest Satan tempt you through lack of self-control.
>
> (1 Cor. 7:3-5)

Paul tells us here that a husband and wife are actually obligated to be available to one another for sexual relations. He doesn't speak in terms of the husband's headship or the wife's submission: neither husband nor wife has rights over his or her own body. They are each responsible for fulfilling the other's desires.

This means that the husband commits himself to be available to his wife even when he feels tired or irritable or would rather watch television. A wife commits herself to the same degree of availability. Each partner should be able to rely upon the other even in discouraging circumstances.

Of course, this commitment must be balanced by genuine concern and love. Just because a husband knows that his wife is committed to meeting his desires, he shouldn't demand intercourse when she is exhausted by a long day of work or sick with the flu. The commitment must also be expressed joyfully, not in a begrudging or purely dutiful spirit. Nothing is more discouraging for a husband or wife asking for his or her marital rights than to be met with, "Okay, I know I have a commitment. Go ahead." The sexual commitment of marriage is based on love, and love should be the spirit in which we fulfill it.

When balanced by concern and willingness, a couple's commitment to be available to each other will spare them a great deal of tension and misunderstanding. Without commitment neither partner knows for sure what to expect: "What mood will she be in tonight?" "Will he want to go right to sleep?" The little signals they send each other may be missed, even ignored.

The absence of commitment also opens a couple's sexual relationship up to manipulation and power plays. The wife who gets her own way by withholding intercourse from her husband has been a subject for humorists as far back as ancient Greece, and it is not uncommon for husbands to try the same tactics. Manipulation of this kind can prove deadly in a marriage, where husband and wife have given up much of the independence and self-reliance that usually defend us against hurt.

After talking to many married couples about sexual commitment, I have seen the effect such a commitment can have. I have seen individuals plagued by sexual problems—an obsession with masturbation or pornography or lust for another person—put those problems behind them once they established a dependable, regular sexual relationship with their marriage partners. The Lord wants to bring that kind of healing to all married couples. He wants to heal us of any dispersion of our sexual energies so that we can focus them fully on our relationship with the one person we have married.

Chaste

"Chaste" may seem an odd word to use when discussing sexual relations in marriage. We usually associate it with the word "celibate"—abstaining completely from sexual intercourse. That is not at all the meaning I intend here:

marriage is *not* a celibate relationship, and excepting the most unusual circumstances, it should not be conducted as one. The reason I use the word "chaste" is because it has a broader meaning—freedom from any kind of immoral or lustful behavior.

Even given that broader definition, some Christians see no need to speak about chastity in a discussion of marriage. In their eyes, a husband and wife have absolutely no bounds on their sexual conduct. Once two people are married, they can do anything they want for sexual pleasure. Except for the one stipulation that the couple be married (and some Christians will not insist even on that), this attitude could come straight from the manuals of the sexual revolution.

Scripture, however, tells married Christians to conduct their sexual lives differently from people who live as pagans in the world: "For this is the will of God: . . . that each one of you know how to take a wife for himself in holiness and honor, not in the passion of lust like heathen who do not know God" (1 Thess. 4:3-5). There is, in other words, a certain decorum appropriate between husband and wife in a Christian marriage. Scripture does not call us to a false modesty based on shame about our bodies or about sex, but it does demand that husband and wife have a basic respect for one another and for God's intentions in creating us sexual beings.

One way to see what this respect involves is to look at the specific question of variety in sexual expression. A couple should have enough freedom in their sexual relations to allow for a reasonable degree of variety and experimentation. This "reasonable degree' of variety might for some couples include trying different positions for intercourse or making manual or oral stimulation of the genitals a part of foreplay. But as we have already seen, Christian thought also maintains that a sexual act should culminate in genital intercourse, the penis in the vagina.

Other types of intercourse, which violate the created design of our sexual faculties, would not be appropriate even for husband and wife.

So chastity in marriage does not rule out variety in sexual expression. It simply calls us to respect certain basic Christian guidelines for the conduct that is appropriate in our relationship. This sense of what is appropriate would extend also to the way a husband and wife talk about sex and act toward one another. Certainly they can talk freely about sex and delight in each other's bodies, but at the same time they should maintain the respect and purity that are appropriate in all Christian life.

Centered on Christ

Finally, the most distinctive element of a sexual relationship based on Christian attitudes is Christ himself. Christian marriage does not depend on compatibility or natural attraction or the "pleasure bond," but on the love of Christ poured into our hearts by the Holy Spirit. There are entirely different realities at work than our limited human ability to love—even in our sexual relationship.

A Christian husband has the power of Christ enabling him to serve his wife sexually in a way that builds her up, gives her joy, refreshes and comforts her, satisfies her physical desire. He can express to her sexually the same quality of love that led Christ to give his life for his people. And the Christian wife in turn can give herself to her husband with the trust and abandonment that marks the church's response to Christ. Just as God's people do not simply receive Christ's love passively, but are moved by it to give themselves completely to him, so a wife moved by God's Spirit can respond eagerly and joyfully to her husband's sexual initiative, returning support and encouragement and refreshment and pleasure just as she receives them.

Of course, a husband will not make a sudden leap into

the full maturity of sexual love, nor will the wife achieve in one moment a mature, wholehearted response. A process of growth in the giving of sexual love must go on constantly, throughout the years of marriage. Nevertheless, it is a process that even from the beginning draws us more deeply into the reality of Christian marriage—a covenant love that joins us together in unity with one another and with Christ.

Sexual relations express and renew this covenant; at the same time, they are a natural human function. As such, sex has nothing inherently mystical about it. We should not be looking for tangible spiritual experiences or a special sense of God's presence as a normal part of sexual relations. Yet natural human experiences, when done in conformity to God's will, serve as means of experiencing his blessing and love.

In the end, the general attitude a Christian couple should have toward their sexual relationship is gratitude. No matter how far we might have to go in overcoming sexual problems, we should never lose sight of the fact that simply being able to be close to each other physically, touch one another, kiss, hold hands, have intercourse, is in itself a gift of no small value from our Father in heaven.

CHAPTER SEVEN

ESTABLISHING THE
SEXUAL RELATIONSHIP

As I mentioned in the last chapter, one tendency of the modern sex manual is to reduce love-making to a matter of technique. But it takes a lot more than technique to create a rewarding sex life. Sex in marriage is primarily a relationship between husband and wife, a relationship designed not only to produce physical stimulation, but also to express love.

A couple's sexual relationship involves their emotions, minds, and spirits as well as their bodies. They need to devote a certain amount of time and attention to building a close relationship, and once it is established, they have to take steps to ensure that the relationship continues to grow. They must always be learning more about each other; they must always be adjusting to problems that appear or new circumstances that affect them.

The basic attitudes toward sex that I discussed in the last chapter are important to the success of a couple's sexual relationship. But there are also many practical elements involved, as in any love relationship. Time, communication, practical knowledge—a couple has to pay attention to these things if they want to establish and maintain a satisfying sexual relationship.

Some practical considerations are so fundamental to the sexual relationship that a couple has to take active concern

for them from the very beginning. That is true whether
they are a newly married couple just establishing their
sexual relationship, or a couple trying to re-establish a relationship that has been unsatisfactory for years. The considerations include learning about each other's sexual responses, determining how often to have intercourse,
agreeing on what sexual behavior is appropriate, and facing the question of family planning. One other practical
element is tied up with all of these, and may be the most
important of all—communication.

Despite the very open climate for sexual discussion that
now exists in our society, many husbands and wives still
find it difficult to be open with each other about sex. Yet
without open communication, there is simply no way for
one partner to understand what the other experiences in
their sexual relationship. There is no way to settle even
simple problems they encounter. A couple who will discuss their sexual feelings honestly and freely have gone a
long way toward building a strong, satisfying relationship.

Usually, however, the best time to talk about sex is not
right in the middle of making love, but during time set
aside specifically for communication. The principles for
communication that were presented in an earlier chapter
can all apply to communication about sex.

Learning About Each Other

One of the practical elements that go into a sexual relationship is simple knowledge about each other. Each husband needs to know what kind of person his wife is
sexually—her feelings and attitudes about sex, what she
finds stimulating and what she dislikes. Each wife needs
the same knowledge about her husband. Many of the problems that couples encounter with sex stem from ignorance
of what they each want and need.

Most couples learn quickly that there are big differences

in their individual sexual responses. Men and women in general respond differently; any two individuals respond differently. Sometimes these differences seem like obstacles, but they can become a real asset to the relationship once we learn to understand and respect them.

Some differences in sexual response seem to be keyed to basic differences between men and women. A man can usually be aroused very quickly, almost automatically, by direct stimulation—touching his wife, or seeing her undress, or getting into bed with her. His sexual response may not depend a great deal on the rest of his relationship with his wife; he can often be aroused almost independently of his feelings or emotions.

A woman's sexual response seems to be more closely tied to her overall emotions. Women tend to be stimulated gradually rather than immediately, and the amount of tenderness and affection they receive during the day—not just at bedtime—will affect their sexual response. A woman's response also has more to do with her whole relationship with her husband. Factors like good communication, warmth, and closeness in the marriage can be as important as direct physical stimulation.

Differences between men and women are not absolutes—each person's sexual feelings are unique. But most couples find themselves affected to some degree or another by differences like these. Often, these differences lie behind problems that a couple encounters.

For example, a man might barely speak to his wife when he gets home from work, but then be surprised that she doesn't immediately respond when he tries to initiate intercourse. His wife's response, however, is perfectly normal for a woman who doesn't see any affection until the moment her husband shuts the bedroom door. Many women who have trouble experiencing much enjoyment or pleasure in intercourse complain of husbands who fail to express love in the rest of their life together. One wife

told me, "When it's time to go to sleep, my husband just
rolls over and doesn't even say good-night. It leaves me
feeling unloved."

Husbands need to learn how to show affection to their
wives at other times than when they get in bed. The fact
that they have a sexual relationship based on a commitment to be available does not mean they can dispense with
sensitivity and love. I know one husband who decided
never to go to sleep without first kissing his wife good
night. Just these ordinary ways of expressing affection can
make a real difference for a woman's sexual response.

Frequency

The question of how often a couple should have intercourse causes considerable tension in many marriages.
One partner complains that the other never wants to have
intercourse, while that partner is exasperated by the first's
demands. I have no intention of setting a rule for how
often a married couple should make love, but I can offer
some general guidelines to help couples consider this issue.

Paul's instructions on sexual relations in the first letter
to the Corinthians speak clearly about the importance of
regular intercourse in marriage: "Do not refuse one
another except perhaps by agreement for a season, that
you may devote yourselves to prayer; but then come together again, lest Satan tempt you through lack of self-
control" (1 Cor. 7:5). Marriage is meant to satisfy our sexual needs by providing regular sexual activity. When a
couple doesn't have intercourse regularly, one or the other
partner, or both, will likely be more susceptible to sexual
temptation. It is easier to live in complete celibacy than to
be in a sexual relationship that is not reasonably regular.

A couple with any question about how often they should
have intercourse should ask, "Do we have intercourse

often enough to maintain a satisfying sexual relationship?" I have found that the more common problem among busy, committed Christians is that they do not. Often their sexual relationship is too irregular to fulfill its purpose in their marriage.

How can a couple determine the right frequency of intercourse for their relationship?

Some ancient Jewish teachers tried to answer this question by considering the particular circumstances of different ways of life. The Babylonian Talmud, a compilation of Jewish law and custom written shortly after the birth of Christ, tried to specify the correct frequency for people according to their professions. Unemployed laborers were to have intercourse with their wives every day; students, twice a week; camel-drivers, once every two weeks; sailors, once a month; and so on.

Obviously, no Christian couple is bound to follow the standards of the Babylonian Talmud. But a husband and wife should talk together about their sexual life and agree on the frequency best for them. They can consider such factors as, What are my personal sexual needs? Is our sexual relationship growing? Is it meeting our needs? What other circumstances in our life affect my sexual desires— does work often leave me too exhausted to make love?

The goal here is not to set up weekly quota for their sexual life, but to determine, as a couple, what they need for a satisfying sexual relationship. Circumstances may occasionally prevent a couple from having intercourse as frequently as they had judged appropriate, but that is not a big problem. It is not so important to actually have intercourse some precise number of nights, but to have intercourse regularly enough to constitute a real sexual relationship.

Once a couple determines the frequency right for their relationship, they may find some rough scheduling helpful in maintaining it. The idea of introducing any scheduling into our sex lives may sound like the death of all spontaneity. But important as spontaneity is, a couple sometimes just has to make sure that they have enough time in their lives to make love. If a busy husband and wife leave everything in their sexual relationship to spontaneity, they may find that they don't have intercourse very often. Few couples actually need a regular schedule for sexual intercourse, but every couple has to pay enough attention to scheduling to ensure that other activities and commitments do not crowd out the time they need for an adequate sexual relationship.

Sexual Expression

Ten or twenty years ago, the question of what types of sexual expression a couple found acceptable for their relationship might never have arisen. But with all the emphasis now placed upon sexual experimentation, I think it is wise for a couple to be able to communicate their feelings on this question. The tension that arises when one partner wants to try things that the other feels uncomfortable with can be a serious problem in their relationship.

In the last chapter, I offered some guidelines for the type of sexual expression appropriate to a Christian marriage. I don't have anything to add here on that point, but I do encourage couples to discuss this issue as one of the fundamental practical elements of their relationship.

Family Planning

The primary biological function of intercourse is to bring the ovum and sperm together. And that means that any discussion of the practical elements of a couple's sexual relationship has to take family planning into account. With modern methods of birth control, it is now possible to avoid pregnancy completely, but I believe that a couple capable of having children should usually have them. It seems obvious that God meant marriage to result in children, and the deliberately childless marriage seems out of line with his design.

A couple should, however, take responsibility for how many children they have. Almost all the major churches— including the Catholic Church—agree that parents have a responsibility for the size of their family. Pope Paul's encyclical on family planning, *Humanae Vitae*, states:

> In relation to physical, economic, psychological and social conditions, responsible parenthood is exercised, either by the deliberate and generous decision to raise a numerous family, or by the decision, made for grave motives and with due respect for the moral law, to avoid for the time being, or even for an indeterminate period, a new birth.[1]

The difference between Catholic and Protestant positions on family planning has to do with the means of birth control; *Humanae Vitae* accepted only those forms of birth control that rely on the natural fertility cycle. However, recent research into natural family planning has produced some highly effective methods, so that Catholics can find reliable means of birth control that conform to the official church teaching.

I occasionally run across Christians who tell me that they don't do anything about family planning because they trust God to give them the right number of children. That might sound good, but unless the couple is really prepared to raise a large family, their words may cloak a basic irresponsibility. Ordinarily, a man responsible for his family's welfare is not supposed to sit back and say, "Oh, I'm going to trust God to bring the money in." He is supposed to

1. *Humanae Vitae*, n. 10.

work to the best of his ability to earn that money. He can trust God to provide him with a job, to give him the strength to do his work, and to care for his family if he cannot work. But he needs to take a personal responsibility for earning his family's income.

In the same way, a married couple should take responsibility to discuss their family size seriously, weigh the factors involved in having more children, and take appropriate steps to avoid conception if they see a need to limit their family. A number of factors enter into decisions like these. For one thing, changing social conditions have erased many of the advantages a big family once had. Children used to be a sizeable economic advantage. They could work on the family farm or take a job to bring in extra income. They were also the parents' sole economic resource in old age. Today, however, a large family costs a lot, but does not insure more income.

Also in the past, many children died as infants. A couple who had twelve children might see only five or six live to adulthood. Most children born today, at least in developed countries, will survive childhood. So it takes fewer births to produce a sizeable family.

Finally, there may be valid reasons for concern about world overpopulation. Although statements on this problem are often exaggerated, it remains true that the world's population has jumped very quickly from one to four billion, which puts a big strain on our resources. If resources were more evenly distributed, the problem might be less severe. But as it is, many people are already hungry and controlling population growth may have to play some part in preventing future famines.

It would seem that many factors in our current situation favor smaller families. Yet Scripture does present children—numerous children—as a blessing from God. I can see good reasons for Christian families in particular to continue to have large families.

For one thing, I think that even with the threat of over-population the world could use more Christian children. Christian parents who have their own lives in order before the Lord are well equipped to raise strong, well-adjusted children who can further God's work in the world. Society itself desperately needs more healthy, balanced children to avoid a future of amorality and lawlessness. There can never be too many children being raised in the kingdom of God as servants of Christ.

It also seems that children play a part in God's plan for building up the church. It may seem funny to speak of having children as a form of evangelism, but it is a very real way in which the church grows. One reason why the Catholic Church has become the largest Christian body in the world is that it has encouraged large families.

As a couple weighs these factors for and against a large family, they also need to consider their personal resources. One important question is simply how large a family they can afford. With the cost of clothing, feeding, doctoring, housing and schooling a child going up, some families just can't afford very many children. On the other hand, there is an important place for trust in God's provision for our needs. Some couples find that by freely choosing a simpler lifestyle they can afford a larger family than they first thought.

Some couples also seem better equipped for parenthood than others. There are parents who seem able to do a great job raising a lot of children, and others who find parenthood more difficult. Those couples who make exceptional parents should consider having a larger family.

One other personal factor to bear in mind is that God may call a couple to some mission in life that will affect the number of children they can raise. Having children is not the only form of evangelism, and God may call some couples to put their time and energy into endeavors that mean limiting their family size. For example, if it really seems that God wants a father in some career that involves frequent travelling, the parents should perhaps consider not having a large family.

In trying to think about all these factors and make a decision about family size, couples should remember that they don't need to decide all at once how many children they are going to have. To the best of my knowledge, the Lord doesn't line newlyweds up and say, "Okay, it's three for you, five for you, two for you." God's guidance seems to come child by child, and I encourage couples to make their family planning decisions child by child. If they do well with their first child, feel right about having another and are in the circumstances to do so, they should have a second. And if it again seems right to have another, then they should have a third. Each decision should be based on careful consideration of all the factors involved and on whatever guidance the Lord offers.

What about an unexpected pregnancy? After all, the only guaranteed means of birth control is total abstention from intercourse. Whether through the fault of the couple or the method they are using, unplanned pregnancies do happen.

There is a tendency to think of unplanned pregnancy as an accident. But in God's eyes, no human life is really accidental. The children we don't plan can bring us just as much joy as those we do if we accept them in a spirit of thankfulness and trust. We don't have to feel that we have messed up God's plan for our life if we end up with more children than might have seemed ideal. In everything, including this, God works things out for the best for those who love him.

CHAPTER EIGHT

IMPROVING THE SEXUAL RELATIONSHIP

No matter how long a couple has had their sexual relationship established, problems are likely to arise between them from time to time. Most of these problems will be fairly simple matters which get resolved without too much trouble. But occasionally, a couple may experience much more difficult problems that seriously threaten their relationship.

A few generations ago, a couple with any kind of sexual problem had few resources to help them do anything about it. There weren't any books available that discussed sex in helpful terms; doctors and ministers had little advice to offer; social taboos made it difficult for a husband and wife even to admit to each other that they were having difficulties.

Today, of course, it takes a special effort to sort out advice consistent with Christian principles from the proliferation of material available. But at least help is there. A couple having problems with sex can usually find a solution if they make the effort.

There are some basic principles that a Christian husband and wife can follow as they seek a solution for problems in their sexual relationship. First of all, they should get the problem out into the light. They should talk about it, tell each other what they are feeling or experiencing. No problem can be resolved when it is hidden.

Sometimes when the problem is in the light where it can be discussed, the couple will find that it is not really a sexual problem. All kinds of personal problems can create tensions or frustrations that surface in sexual relations. Perhaps a couple are not communicating well, or the husband is neglecting the children, or they have financial trouble. One woman discovered that she wasn't able to have a satisfying sexual relationship with her husband until she had dealt with resentments she felt toward her father for past wrongs.

Of course, the problem might prove to be purely sexual. A couple can have an excellent marriage overall, but still have difficulties in sex. But no matter where the root of the problem lies—whether in the marriage as a whole or specifically in the sexual relationship—the only way to get at it is to bring the matter into the open where it can be discussed.

Once the problem is in the light, a couple should ask the Lord for wisdom in searching for a solution. A Christian husband and wife don't have to face any problem alone. Sometimes we hesitate to ask the Lord's help in sexual matters. We ask him to help us raise our children or communicate with each other or balance the budget, but we can't quite believe that he really cares about our sexual lives. Well, God does care. Sex is a gift from him, and he wants to teach us how to conduct this part of our lives too.

Finally, as a couple tries to work through a problem, they should keep a long-range perspective. Sexual difficulties may need some time to clear up completely; one of the worst things that can happen in the meantime is to be under pressure to see a change.

When a couple needs to deal with some problem in their sexual relationship, I usually suggest that they decide on the steps they will take, but then not try to analyze their progress for several months. It is not going to help them to keep looking over their shoulders to see if things are improving. They should take the steps they decide upon, put the problem out of their minds, and then, after some time has passed, talk the matter over again and see where things stand.

If a problem persists, or if a couple need help getting their bearings on how to deal with it, they should talk with a responsible, mature Christian who has had some experience in dealing with marriage problems. The counselor should be someone who can be trusted to offer both a truly Christian outlook and sound marital advice.

With this basic approach to dealing with sexual problems in mind, I would like to discuss a few of the specific problems that can develop in a couple's relationship and offer some guidelines for dealing with them.

Adjustment

Because a husband and wife do respond to sex differently, they need to make certain adjustments to each other to have a successful sexual relationship. A newly married couple particularly needs time to become familiar with one another's responses and get used to relating sexually. This initial adjustment varies with each couple: with some it seems almost automatic, while others need quite a long time.

Problems can arise during a period of adjustments if the two partners don't tell each other their true feelings about the relationship. Sometimes the husband or the wife would like to change something in the way they make love, but is afraid to say so. The other partner can go on for years without knowing that her husband thinks she is too demanding or that his wife wishes he would take more time for foreplay.

Other periods of adjustment may be necessary as the

circumstances surrounding a couple's sexual relationship change. For example, pregnancy and childbirth can affect a woman's sexual responses. The fatigue and discomfort that some women experience in the first and last months of pregnancy may cause a lessening of sexual desire, while the middle months may be a time of increased desire. Some women find that they have a greater interest in sex during the first months after recovery from childbirth, while others find the demands of caring for a newborn leave little time or energy for sex. Obviously, pregnancy and childbirth do not affect every woman in the same way, but a couple should not be disturbed if they experience fluctuations in desire during that time.

Again, menopause has a big impact on a woman's sexual response. Many women find an increase in sexual desire at this time, while their husbands may experience a slight lessening of sexual capacity at about the same age. If these shifts occur, there is no cause for alarm, but the couple will need to make new adjustments in their relationship.

The most important thing to remember during any period of adjustment is to stay in communication. A wife has to tell her husband if she needs more time to get fully aroused; he has to tell her if he has trouble making love late at night. For either to pretend that everything is wonderful when it isn't does a disservice to them both.

Premature Ejaculation

Just as men become sexually aroused very quickly, they often reach a climax quickly once intercourse begins. This can become a problem when a husband regularly has his orgasm so early in intercourse that he cannot maintain an erection long enough for intercourse to be a satisfying experience for his wife. This "premature ejaculation" both deprives the wife of the pleasure she would normally receive and causes the husband anxiety about his sexual adequacy. Ironically, anxiety can actually cause premature ejaculation, and so the whole problem is aggravated.

The key to overcoming premature ejaculation often lies in learning to relax. A more leisurely period of foreplay can be very helpful here. Longer foreplay helps both partners relax; it helps the wife become more fully aroused, so that she can reach her climax more easily; and, almost paradoxically, it can lessen the chance of an immediate ejaculation when intercourse begins.

Controlling the pace of intercourse can be a help. Rapid thrusting movements give the penis maximum stimulation and will bring a man to his climax very quickly. A man who wishes to delay his orgasm may find it helpful to remain still for a short while immediately after entry, and then pause again whenever ejaculation seems imminent. He can also use a slower rhythm and fewer thrusting motions during intercourse.

Having intercourse regularly may also make a difference. After a long period of abstinence, intercourse may initially be so stimulating as to cause a premature ejaculation. Some men have found lying on their sides during intercourse helpful, using a position recommended by Dr. John Eichenlaub in his book *The Marriage Art* (available as a Dell paperback, published 1969). And age and experience have helped others. Often the solution is just a matter of growing out of old habits of solitary sexual experience into the mutuality of married sex.

Premature ejaculation need not remain a serious problem in a couple's sexual relationship. With patience and time it can almost always be overcome.

The Orgasm Controversy

An enormous controversy has developed in recent years over a problem that used to be called "frigidity" and is now usually termed "orgasmic impairment." Both of these terms refer to women who are unable to reach a satisfying climax in sexual intercourse. This problem is a reason for genuine concern, but unfortunately, the research being done on it has become so polemical as to stop being very helpful.

For one thing, every researcher seems to reach a different conclusion about the real source and nature of female orgasm. One claims that stimulation of the clitoris during intercourse causes orgasm, another insists that clitoral orgasms are infantile and true orgasm centers on the vagina, yet another announces that intercourse itself cannot give women an orgasm in the first place. With so much confusion still surrounding the matter, one would expect researchers to be rather cautious in stating their conclusions. But instead each new study is more dogmatic in its statement than the last.

The whole question has also been taken up by the women's liberation movement, which sees it in terms of male oppression, so now we have politics on top of confusion. The end result of all this controversy is an enormous preoccupation with the intensity and quality of a woman's sexual experience. Many women feel under pressure to live up to the experiences that someone else presents as a norm for sexual fulfillment.

In such a highly charged atmosphere, what is a Christian couple to do when the wife cannot experience a satisfactory level of enjoyment in their sexual relationship? The first thing I would suggest is that they resist the pressure to make a particular type of orgasm their goal—or a certain number of orgasms, or even having an orgasm at all. The fact is that the physical experience called orgasm varies a lot according to individual women and particular circumstances. British researchers have stated:

There is no such thing as an "average" orgasm, and it is almost impossible to describe an orgasm, since it varies from person to person and from one sexual intercourse to the next in the same woman. Orgasm can be an explosive experience lasting from three to four seconds to about ten seconds for the ultimate release of a high degree of tension. When lesser degrees of tension are created, orgasm may be a sudden suffusion of warmth of a less explosive nature—merely a pleasant, loving, cosy emotion . . . the intensity of any particular orgasm varies for many reasons, such as the time in the menstrual cycle, anxiety or excessive fatigue, extremely hot weather . . . or most important, just the way she feels about making love at that particular time . . . Some women never have more than a mild climax that is merely relaxing and scarcely discernible as such . . .[1]

Given the fact that the experience of orgasm varies so much, a couple would be wise to stop trying to achieve a particular physical sensation, and concentrate instead on growing in the enjoyment and satisfaction they find in their sexual relationship. Do they both take joy and delight in their sexual relationship? Do they experience intercourse as a sharing of love and affection? Do they find it physically pleasurable and satisfying? It may well be that upon considering these questions, both husband and wife will see room for growth in their ability to enjoy sex. Most of us have not reached our full potential in dozens of areas, from enjoying intercourse to playing tennis.

If the wife is not finding the couple's sexual relationship enjoyable and satisfying, the couple can take some reasonable steps that may help her. First, they should be sure to express love in all of their life together. As I have mentioned before, tenderness and affection play an important part in a woman's sexual response. The husband should be especially careful to show his affection for his wife at all

1. Maxine Davis, *Sexual Responsibility in Marriage* (Fontana Books, London: twelfth printing, 1976), pp. 170-174.

times, both within sexual intercourse and in ordinary events of their life.

To create an atmosphere of love and affection, a couple may also need to solve other problems in the marriage. The only case of severe orgasmic impairment I have encountered in the last few years of counseling married couples was directly related to hostile feelings that a woman had developed toward her husband. It was basically a problem in their personal relationship, not in their sex life. When a couple maintains an attitude of committed love and service, expressing that attitude through tenderness and consideration, both partners usually find sex enjoyable and satisfying.

Growth in sexual satisfaction may also depend on resolving bad attitudes about sex. Fear of men, feelings of guilt or shame, and bad memories of past sexual experiences can all keep a woman from fully enjoying intercourse with her husband. Good communication about sex can help bring these problems to the surface where the couple can begin to deal with them.

The circumstances surrounding a couple's lovemaking give another key to growth. Some couples need to allow more time in their love-making for foreplay and gentle expressions of tenderness. Or a woman may find that she enjoys intercourse more if it follows a time spent talking with her husband in a relaxed, intimate setting. Sometimes a couple needs to allow more time for rest, so that neither partner is too tired to enjoy making love. When circumstances permit it, a couple may prefer to have intercourse in the morning or afternoon, when they feel more rested and alert.

Worries about privacy or fear of getting pregnant can also affect a couple's sexual relations. If they are afraid that neighbors in the next apartment will hear their creaking bedsprings, they can try making a bed on the floor. If the children might come barging in, they should keep the bedroom door locked. If they don't wish to become pregnant at a particular time, they should take some responsible steps to avoid conception.

Finally, a woman's inability to enjoy intercourse might be corrected by a better knowledge of sexual physiology. For example, some women have been unable to reach a satisfying climax because neither they nor their husbands understood the role of the clitoris in giving a woman sexual pleasure. Women should tell their husbands freely and honestly what they find stimulating. A couple might also look for a reliable book that explains sexual response and the techniques of intercourse.[2]

Along these lines, research has shown that in some women the muscles surrounding the vagina have been stretched in childbirth or are naturally weak. The muscular weakness may reduce the pleasure these women receive from intercourse. A very simple exercise developed by Dr. Arnold Kegel[3] will strengthen these muscles.

In dealing with any difficulty in a couple's sexual relationship, it is good to remember that sex is only one part of married life. It is important, but it is not the focus of the entire relationship. A couple can have a wonderful sex life, yet still be miserable. Conversely, they can have a happy marriage without ever experiencing the highest possible level of sexual satisfaction.

Most problems in a sexual relationship will yield to patient efforts at growth and improvement. Yet a couple may

2. Three books that I partially recommend for both Christian values and reliable information are *The Freedom of Sexual Love* by Joseph and Lois Bird (Doubleday: 1970), *The Act of Marriage* by Tim and Beverly La Haye (Zondervan: 1976), and *Intended for Pleasure* by Ed and Gaye Wheat (Fleming Revell: 1977). None of these books will be entirely acceptable to all major Christian traditions, nor do I myself recommend them unreservedly, but they are the best recent books available.

3. Most doctors are familiar with the Kegel exercises, and the La Hayes devote one chapter to them in *The Act of Marriage*.

run up against some problems that do not seem to change. Or they may have to devote most of their attention at a particular time to other matters in their life, and bear with some inadequacy in their sexual relationship. But the fact that they cannot immediately experience their maximum potential of sexual pleasure, or even that they may never reach it, does not mean that their marriage has failed. All of us, because of our natural human limitations, will fail to reach our full potential in many endeavors.

In the end, married happiness depends not on number or intensity of sexual experiences, but on a couple's commitment to love and support each other in every part of their life together. Sex, after all, is one of the forms of the present life that is passing away (see 1 Cor. 7:31, Luke 20:34-36). What will endure of our marriages to be carried into the new age is what has been built on faithful, Christ-empowered love, in all the ways that love is lived. With this in mind, I want to turn now to the specific ways husbands and wives live out their marriage commitment.

CHAPTER NINE

THE CHRISTIAN HUSBAND

The Bible speaks of a husband's role in marriage largely in terms of his headship, with a corresponding emphasis on submission for the wife. Many modern Christians find this all very authoritarian. They picture a relationship in which the husband gets to boss his wife around all he wants, while she can only resign herself to silent frustration.

Happily, that is not an accurate picture of the biblical teaching. Christian husbands do exercise real authority in marriage, but when Paul wrote, "Wives, be subject to your husbands as to the Lord," he did not then tell the men, "Order your wives around." He said, "Husbands, love your wives, as Christ loved the church" (Eph. 5:25). According to Paul, the heart of a husband's headship is love. Not just any kind of love, either, but the love that Jesus showed the church.

Paul goes on to describe for husbands what Jesus' love consisted of: ". . . Christ loved the church and gave himself up for her, that he might sanctify her, having cleansed her by the washing of water with the word, that he might present the church to himself in splendor, without spot or wrinkle or any such thing, that she might be holy and without blemish" (Eph. 5:25-27).

Jesus entered the world not to further his own interests,

but to give himself up for his people. A Christian husband must also be prepared to give up his will and interests in order to care for his wife. His love will cost him something, just as Jesus' love cost him something. But the goal of a husband's love is also the same as Jesus': to present his wife to the Lord in splendor—as a strong, happy, peaceful woman, in full possession of her gifts and abilities.

The authority aspect of a husband's headship is rooted in his commitment to self-sacrificial love. A husband takes on a deep responsibility to his wife, a responsibility to see that her whole life goes well and is in good order before the Lord. He needs to have authority over her in order to fulfill it, just as Jesus had authority over his disciples in order to guide and teach and care for them.

To say that a husband's authority is based on responsibility for his wife will not necessarily make it more attractive to the modern mind. Many people now deny that a husband should have any special responsibility for his wife. They claim that such responsibility patronizes women, taking away their sense of self-responsibility so as to keep them dependent on men. According to this view, everyone should have completely independent control of his or her own life; responsibility is just another form of oppression.

I suppose any society that prizes independence as much as ours would find responsibility patronizing. But within the body of Christ, especially within a Christian marriage, unity and not independence is the goal. One of the clearest messages of the New Testament is that Christians are not independent, but bound together in a common life as members of one body. They are not supposed to zealously guard control of their own lives; they are called to open their lives up to each other in an attitude of mutual submission.

That context gives responsibility and authority a very different meaning from what it has in our society. A wife submits to her husband not because she is somehow unable to care for herself—it actually takes a strong, competent woman to fill the role of a Christian wife—but for the sake of unity in their common life. In turn, the husband's responsibility for his wife commits him to seeing that within their common life she has all the support and opportunities she needs for her own growth in the Lord.

Such headship is not meant for women only. Husbands also benefit when they can receive personal support and guidance from another man who has authority over them in the Christian community. In fact, I think that a man can best learn to take responsibility for his wife when he himself is under authority. Unfortunately, very few Christian churches are able to offer their members much personal pastoral care. But I believe that husbands can still find many ways to practice submission in their own lives.

They can begin by submitting themselves fully to the Lord. In the time they spend praying and reading Scripture, their attitude should be, "Lord, I want to lay down my own will for my life and submit to you. Show me what your will is, and I will accept it." They can also look for opportunities to receive some personal headship within their church or perhaps in a local prayer group. This calls for a certain amount of caution: men should not rush out to submit themselves to just anyone who offers his authority. But there are Christian groups that offer a fuller degree of responsible pastoral care, while respecting and supporting their members' church and family commitments.

For the husband's authority and responsibility to mean anything, they have to make some practical difference in the way he and his wife live. He must express his love for her by actually caring for her and fulfilling his responsibilities in the home. I want to go on now to discuss what a husband can do practically to love his wife as Jesus loved the church.

Service

Jesus set a model for leadership among Christians: "Let the greatest among you become as the youngest, and the leader as one who serves. For ... I am among you as one who serves" (Luke 22:26-27). Within the body of Christ, those who exercise authority are first and foremost the servants of those under them. This truth applies to the Christian husband in his relationship with his wife: as one who has authority, he is also called to serve.

The word servant may conjure up thoughts of someone like a butler, who answers the door, waits on the table, and carries in breakfast on a silver tray. That's not quite the type of servant I have in mind. I do not recommend that a husband get a silver tray and start waiting on his wife. By a servant, I mean someone who is ready to spend himself completely in helping and supporting another person.

The primary way a husband serves his wife is by exercising his authority for her good, just as Jesus' greatest service to his disciples was his teaching and direction and personal care. But his commitment to service should also extend to the practical details of the life he shares with his wife. For example, most husbands are responsible for earning at least a major portion of the family income. When a man works faithfully to provide for his family's needs, he shows that he is a servant.

Unfortunately, many men seem to think their duty to serve stops with their paychecks. They work hard to support their families and think nothing more should be expected of them. I would not underrate the importance of earning a living, but I do encourage husbands to recognize their broader responsibilities as servants.

A good place to start is with chores around the house.

Every husband has certain duties of his own in the home, usually things like car maintenance, house repairs, yard work, the family finances. It is very frustrating for wives to have to push their husbands to get these chores done. Men often complain about nagging wives, but they should ask themselves, "How often do I cause my wife's nagging by my own lack of faithfulness?"

Another responsibility that many husbands ignore is child-rearing. Fewer and fewer fathers play any significant part in their children's upbringing, so their wives carry the burden of being two parents at once. A man should get involved with his children—talking to them, playing with them, spending time with them. As a father, he has a special responsibility to discipline the children and train them in Christian life. He also has special responsibility for the boys in the family, who need his formative influence to help establish their own identity as men. Particularly as boys get up above the age of six, their fathers should be actively involved in their training and formation.

One other way a husband shows himself a servant is by a general attitude of helpfulness and concern at home. When his wife gets in a real pinch with her own responsibilities—say he comes home to find dinner burning and the children crying and his wife exhausted—he should offer to help rather than retire to the living room with his paper. If the kids need help with school work, he can volunteer rather than always leave it to his wife. These are very simple ways of showing concern, but they do serve as signs of a man's love for his family and his determination to care for them.

Practical Direction

One of the greatest services a husband can perform for his wife is to take an active responsibility for her daily life.

A modern wife faces many demanding, sometimes be-wildering, responsibilities. Running a household—and I'm talking about an average household with cooking and cleaning and telephone calls and children—is in itself a complex task. On top of it come all the demands of service in a church or prayer group, volunteer work, a job, or any of the other responsibilities that women are expected to handle.

It is quite a challenge to balance so many tasks and still stay on top of one's basic responsibilities. Yet many women face this challenge alone and unprepared. In ear-lier times, a newly married couple usually stayed in close contact with parents and other relatives, so that a wife received a lot of help from her mother and sisters and aunts and cousins as she learned to organize her house-hold. Today the extended family has largely disappeared; a young couple may not even live in the same town as their parents. A woman gets married, moves into her new home, and is suddenly supposed to know all about running a house and caring for children.

The average husband, meanwhile, probably never dreams that he has any responsibility to help his wife keep her daily life in order. He usually knows even less than she about running a house, and figures that it is up to her to work it all out. If his wife has trouble keeping the house clean or preparing the meals or watching children or hold-ing down a job, the most he will ever contribute will be an occasional complaint that the furniture needs dusting.

A husband who wants to provide headship for his wife must be prepared to take an active concern for her daily tasks and duties. Her work, whether in the home or out-side it, is not her responsibility alone, somehow separate from his own concerns. It is an important part of the com-mon life they share together.

He need not know all the ins and outs of his wife's housekeeping or other tasks in order to provide her with helpful direction. His role is in some ways like that of a manager in a business office, and a good manager does not always know exactly how to do every job in the office himself. Management consists of such things as defining responsibility, so that each worker knows exactly what jobs to do; supervising the work flow, so that no one ends up with too much work at one time; and setting priorities, so that people know which of their tasks are most important in case of a schedule conflict.

There are important differences between the way a manager relates to workers and the way a husband relates to his wife: husband and wife are *not* boss and worker. But a husband can do many of the things a manager would do in terms of taking an active concern for his wife's work. And just as a good manager can bring a great deal of peace and order to a busy office, a husband can bring greater peace and order to his wife's busy routine.

To begin with, a husband should help his wife define her responsibilities and establish the right priorities for her time. Many women get bogged down in their work simply because they try to do too much. The husband can help his wife sort through her activities and determine what she should really be doing. It is his responsibility as head of the family to determine which activities are important to their common life and responsibilities and which are not.

A husband should also be concerned to help his wife organize her activities efficiently. Together they can work out a reasonable schedule for her weekly routine. A schedule will give the wife the means to stay in control of her time and activities, and keep them from controlling her.

Putting a schedule together involves listing all the things the wife has to do during the week, figuring out how much time each task will take and when it can be done. The couple should include time for communication between themselves, time for the children, daily time for prayer and Scripture reading, and free time for recreation and personal projects. It is best, however, not to schedule up every moment in the week. (You may wonder how anyone can possibly fit all that in without scheduling up more than a week. I can tell you from experience that it *is* possible.) There should be enough leeway to account for chores that take longer than planned or the occasional emergency that throws a whole day's work off.

Although I am speaking here primarily about a husband's responsibilities to his wife, I want to point out that practical direction of this kind is equally important for husbands. Men also have trouble keeping their activities and schedules in good order. If some degree of personal pastoral care is available to a husband, his head can help him sort out his responsibilities and establish a reasonable weekly schedule, in much the same way he would help his wife. In addition, even if the husband cannot find personal headship within the local Christian community, he should discuss his schedule and responsibilities with his wife. He can then coordinate his activities with hers and get her input on his priorities and commitments.

Whatever a couple determines about their schedules and responsibilities, the husband must support his wife as they work to implement the decisions. He cannot say, "Take an hour every day for prayer and Scripture reading," and then leave her to figure out how to handle the children and the phone and the dozen other things that come up during that hour. He needs to see that their life is so arranged that his wife is able to do what they have agreed she should.

In the case of finding time for prayer, he may need to say, "Take the phone off the hook for that hour. Your prayer time is more important to our common life than the telephone." Or perhaps he will need to take care of the children for an hour every evening so that she has an undisturbed time for prayer. Whatever the practical solution turns out to be, the important thing is that the husband take responsibility to see that his wife's schedule works.

The point in all of this is not that women are incapable of organizing their own time. Many women do an excellent job of managing their homes and a great many other activities. Often they can teach their husbands a lot about organization. But whether a wife is extremely capable or still needs to learn the basics of organization, her husband has responsibility for her time and work. That does not necessarily mean that he will dictate her schedule: they should usually work this out together. But he does need to take an active concern both for the good order of her personal life and for the practical needs of their common life.

Spiritual Leadership

Authority in the Christian family extends to more than practical details. The Lord also calls husbands to become spiritual leaders, capable of taking real responsibility for their families' response to him. Scripture portrays many men who were very much the spiritual leaders of their families. One impressive example is Joshua, who could stand before all the people of Israel and commit his household to the ways of God: "as for me and my house, we will serve the Lord" (Josh. 24:15). Another is the centurion Cornelius, whose personal holiness and prayers resulted in his family's becoming the first gentiles to receive the gift of the Holy Spirit (Acts 10).

From what I have seen in counseling married couples and travelling around to speak to Christian groups, I cannot say that the average Christian husband today patterns himself after Joshua and Cornelius. I frequently see women making the rounds of local priests or ministers or prayer group leaders searching for the spiritual leadership they miss at home. An amazing number of Christian husbands have no idea what happens in their wives' relationships with the Lord. Many are simply uninterested; others feel ill at ease with the topic.

Usually, such a husband is delighted when his wife can find a priest or minister or anyone who takes an interest in her spiritual life. Then *he* gets off the hook. He is equally happy to let his wife take charge of any spiritual life within their home—family prayer or Bible study, church attendance, teaching the children how to pray. Somewhere along the line, these husbands have decided that spiritual matters are beyond their competence.

Yet no matter how reluctant to take spiritual leadership a husband may be, he has a responsibility to encourage, support and guide his wife in spiritual matters as well as practical ones. It does not matter that he has yet to reach heroic holiness or acquire all spiritual knowledge. God is perfectly aware of our inadequacies and will give us whatever help we need. But he wants men to step out and begin fulfilling their responsibilities in the home.

Spiritual leadership begins with the husband's own relationship with God. There is no way he can affect his wife's growth in the Lord if his own spiritual life is stagnating. He needs time each day for prayer, time when he can pray both for the needs he and his wife face and for a deeper knowledge and awareness of the Lord himself. Daily Scripture reading is important: it allows God's word to shape the way a man thinks and responds. A husband should also draw on the support and teaching available within his local church, and perhaps within some renewal community, prayer group or smaller fellowship group.

As the husband brings his own spiritual life into order, he will be able to support his wife in her relationship with the Lord. His leadership takes several forms. Most basically, he must be sure that she has sufficient time for regular prayer, Scripture reading, and involvement with other

Christians. Everything that the husband needs for spiritual growth, the wife needs too.

But leadership also means showing active concern for what his wife is experiencing in her spiritual growth. How many husbands know what their wives are learning from Scripture? What happens in their prayer times? What they feel about other people in the church or prayer group? How many are fully aware of what their wives think about themselves and their marriages and their relationships with God? As a spiritual leader, a husband should be able to support and guide his wife in these aspects of her life. To do that, he at least needs to know what is happening to her.

This can be the most difficult aspect of spiritual leadership. Often a husband will not know what to say when his wife tells him she is discouraged about her prayer time or that she feels God wants to change the way she thinks about herself. But he can at least let his wife know that he is concerned and wants to support her. He can encourage her when she is discouraged; he can affirm whatever God is doing to strengthen and teach her; he can take a responsibility for the problems she encounters. If anxiety about some problem keeps her from working peacefully toward a solution, he can call her on to greater trust in God. At times when she feels worthless, he can assure her of her great value in his eyes and in the Lord's eyes. Often, what a wife needs most in terms of spiritual leadership are these simple words of support that show her husband's concern and sense of responsibility.

This is the kind of help that men often expect the pastor or prayer group leader to offer their wives, but the husband should normally provide it. I remember a man who came up to some of our community leaders after hearing a teaching we had given. "Boy, my wife has some strong feelings about that teaching," he said. "You guys are going to have a real problem getting through to her. I'm glad you're the ones dealing with it."

I said, "It sounds to me like *you're* the one who has a problem. It's your responsibility to help your wife sort out her reactions to a teaching so that she can accept what the Lord may have for her in it. If you aren't able to help her, or if you have some questions about the teaching yourself, we are available to help you both out. But it's primarily your responsibility."

That does not mean that a pastor or another woman or a professional counselor should never be involved in counseling a married woman. The husband certainly will not have all the answers, and he should feel free to say, "I don't know what to do about this, but let's find out." Then he can provide leadership in seeking counsel from more experienced Christians or in looking for further insights through prayer, study, and discussion.

In exercising spiritual leadership, a husband needs to maintain a clear vision of what God intends for his wife as a Christian woman. Scripture offers a vision of womanly character quite different from most of our cultural images, and that scriptural ideal should be the focus for a husband's encouragement and advice and correction and prayer. The next chapter, directed to wives, discusses Christian womanhood; it can help husbands grasp this vision. Correspondingly, a wife needs to understand the vision for Christian husbands being presented in this chapter in order to support her husband as he takes up his responsibilities.

An individual's growth in Christian maturity usually follows a certain natural progression, which husbands should keep in mind as they try to provide leadership for their wives in personal and spiritual matters. First, a husband can take concern for his wife's basic relationship with God and her attitudes toward herself as a daughter of God.

Then, he may want to give some attention to helping her become confident in her responsibilities within the family. After that, the couple can explore what it means to be co-workers for the gospel outside the home as well as within it, discussing the forms of Christian service appropriate for them as individuals and as a couple. This progression is ordinarily flexible, but it indicates the basic order of priorities in exercising spiritual leadership.

The husband also has responsibility for the spiritual life of the family as a whole. He should make sure that he and his wife stay in good communication about those things they feel the Lord is doing with either of them. Just as he should find out what is happening in his wife's relationship to the Lord, he should be sharing with her what happens in his own spiritual life. And he should take responsibility for any family prayer or Bible study and for the family's involvement in their church and other Christian groups.

Above all, he must be responsible to hear the Lord for his family. He should look for the Lord's guidance in decisions that face the family; he should seek the Lord for direction for the family as a whole.

The husband's spiritual leadership does not leave the wife without any responsibility for the spiritual life of the family. He is responsible for making any final decisions about the family's response to the Lord's word, but that word may come through his wife. He would be wise to encourage her contributions.

Affection and Respect

The spirit in which a husband exercises authority is as important as the actual headship he gives. Does he use his position in the family arrogantly, for his own benefit, or does he use it according to Paul's instruction: "Husbands, love your wives, as Christ loved the church" (Eph. 5:25). If headship is taken out of the context of love, it may become oppressive.

So it is very important that a husband base his authority on a deep love for his wife. Sometimes headship sounds very cold and functional, but Christian marriage should not become cold or purely functional. Headship is meant to operate within a very warm and close relationship. The husband has as much responsibility for this part of married life as for any other. As leader and initiator, he must take responsibility for the expression of love between his wife and himself.

First of all, the husband should be concerned to show tenderness and affection toward his wife. For some reason, men tend to neglect showing affection in marriage. They think their love is evident in the way they provide for their wives and can't see why they should make any more display about it. If their wives complain of feeling unloved, they write it off as over-emotionalism.

Yet a wife's desire to receive more affection from her husband is usually quite legitimate. It may be true that he feels less need for an open display of affection than she, but that just happens to be a difference between them. It is not a sign of emotional instability. The husband should respect his wife's feelings by making a conscious effort, if necessary, to show more affection. His words and actions should constantly assure her of his love.

Along with affection, a husband should show respect for his wife as a woman of God. Our culture often encourages men to feel a certain contempt for women. This lack of respect takes many forms. An exasperated "I'll never understand women" or a crack about women drivers says "Women don't make sense," "Women are incompetent." A wife's work in the home is considered unimportant compared to her husband's job. Anything that women do differently from men is held against them as a sign of weakness or foolishness.

As I said earlier, Scripture can give husbands a very different view of women. The perfect wife of Proverbs (ch. 31) and the Christian women described by Paul (1 Tim. 5:3-10) are strong, competent, faithful, wise, resourceful— to list a very few of their traits. Women's differences from men in temperament, abilities, and interests are not weaknesses, but part of a unique womanly identity. Husband and wife each have characteristics that complement the other when they are united in marriage, giving them a greater strength together than either can possess alone.

A husband should replace any contempt for women he has picked up from our culture with a high regard for their strengths and insights. He should communicate that regard to his wife, showing that he values her and her contribution to their common life. By listening to her when she speaks, respecting her feelings and thoughts, drawing upon her abilities, and entrusting her with responsibilities, he shows his respect for her.

Even the traditional means of showing respect to women—holding doors, seating women at table, helping with their coats, and so on—are important. I know that some people today consider these manners degrading to women, because they make a distinction between women and men. But I believe that the differences between men and women should be recognized and respected, and that it is right for men to show a special regard for their wives specifically as women. In fact, Scripture links the respect a man shows his wife to the efficacy of his prayer life: "You husbands, too, must show consideration for those who share your lives. Treat women with respect ... If you do so, nothing will keep your prayers from being answered" (1 Pet. 3:7 NAB).

Affection and respect make headship work. When a wife

regularly experiences her husband's love and esteem, she will be better able to trust him with authority for her life. When a husband is continually trying to show love and respect for his wife, he will be more alert to any way his headship becomes harsh or domineering. Affection and respect are important elements of love, and headship in marriage ought to build up the love between husband and wife.

Seen all at once, the responsibilities of a Christian husband may seem beyond the abilities of any ordinary male. But I hope that men will not be discouraged from taking a real authority in their families. If they wait until they feel capable of doing everything in this chapter perfectly, they will never begin. I don't know any husband who exercises perfect headship, but I do know many men who have become far better husbands by taking up their responsibilities to the best of their ability and then learning and growing and maturing.

Besides, a Christian husband does not depend completely on his own abilities. He has a relationship with God that will enable him to receive help from the Lord whenever he exhausts his own resources. That is why a husband's personal spiritual life is so important: it is a real source of strength as he faces his responsibilities.

A husband can also look to his wife for help and support. A woman may be a little apprehensive at first about yielding so much of her daily life to her husband's authority. He will have a lot of authority, and she may not be sure how well he will use it. A husband can help his wife in this by assuring her that he wants to be able to love and care for her. He should ask her to let him know what she thinks about the way he uses his headship, assuring her that he will respectfully consider her observations and advice. Her input will be an invaluable aid to him in deciding how to exercise headship.

Finally, the husband should look for support among other Christians. He and his wife should look for other couples who are trying to put these principles to work in their marriages. Christian husbands can help each other a lot by getting together to share their experiences in headship and to counsel one another. And there are many other resources of teaching and guidance available within the larger Christian community that can make up for the husband's personal limitations.

Above all, a man can trust in the fact that God *has* given him the gifts to be a good husband. The husband's role was designed to draw on characteristics and strengths already planted in every man. This gift of Christian manhood will grow stronger as each husband accepts and values it.

CHAPTER TEN

THE CHRISTIAN WIFE

One of the most important passages in Scripture for understanding the role of a Christian wife is the account of the creation of the first woman (Gen. 2:18-24). I talked about this passage in an earlier chapter, but I want to take a closer look here at what it says specifically to wives.

The passage opens with the creation of man and God's decision to give the man a partner. "Then the Lord God said, 'It is not good that the man should be alone; I will make him a helper fit for him' " (2:18). God created all the beasts and birds, bringing them before the man, but "there was not found a helper fit for him. So the Lord God caused a deep sleep to fall upon the man, and while he slept took one of his ribs and closed up its place with flesh; and the rib which the Lord God had taken from the man he made into a woman and brought her to the man" (2:20-22). The man expressed his delight in his new companion and gave her the name "Woman."

It is significant that this account of woman's creation focuses so much on the man. The woman is created for the man. She is made from him and then brought to him. He names her. The very existence of the woman is expressed largely in terms of her relationship to the man. She is a "helper fit for him."

Many women find this understandably hard to swallow. Genesis would apparently deny a woman any value or importance as an individual in her own right. The man is the center of things; he plays the important part; she is just the helper. That is what women think "a helper fit for him" means, and they do not find the idea very appealing.

Yet Scripture is neither denying a woman's personal value nor restricting her to an inferior position when it speaks of her as a helper. For in the kingdom of God, the role of helper is highly honored. Our society only pays attention to the person who is in charge, directing things; we virtually ignore those in supporting positions. This reflects the independent, competitive spirit that rules our society. People in supporting roles are often abused, while those on top advance their own interests at the expense of others.

God sees his people as a united body, with each individual having particular gifts and responsibilities essential to the welfare of the whole (see 1 Cor. 12:12-26). Supportive roles are as necessary to the life of the body as directive roles, and deserve as much esteem. Unless we actually undergo a conversion to this way of seeing things and break with the competitive values that place "my good" above "our good," we will never be able to live out the Christian vision of marriage. We cannot live the life envisioned in the gospel unless we embrace the gospel principle that he who holds on to his own life will lose it, while he who lays down his life in service will find it.

Scripture treats husband and wife as a single unit of the body of Christ. The particular roles it assigns them are designed to help them work together as a unit. Sometimes people think that unity in marriage means that a couple should spend all their time together, do the same things, and in general be as much alike as possible. In fact, however, it is the very differences between husband and wife that enable them to function in unity. The husband, as head, has primary responsibility to set the direction for the family and represent it to the world at large. The wife is primarily responsible for the family's internal life— making a home and caring for the family members. Her support makes possible the life that goes on in the family. Neither of these roles is more important than the other. They are designed to fit together in a unified whole.

The fact that the husband has overall authority in the family does not mean that the wife has no significant degree of authority and responsibility. John Chrysostom, writing in the fifth century, called the wife the "second authority" in the family. Her authority is subordinate to her husband's, but it is nonetheless real and involves considerable responsibilities. To manage a multitude of household concerns, play a significant part in forming the lives of other human beings, and provide stable personal and spiritual support, is a challenge equivalent to the most demanding career outside the home. Both husband and wife should regard her role in the family with the respect they would give to any other demanding and responsible position.

"If the wife's role is truly important," some people say, "why restrict it to women? Why not make family roles interchangeable?" Yet in Scripture we find that the work of supporting life among God's people, even outside the family context, is a special characteristic of Christian womanhood. We can consider Mary, the mother of Jesus, whose willingness to bear and raise a child was essential to God's plan of salvation. The Gospel of Luke mentions the women who travelled with Jesus and his disciples, "assisting them out of their means" (Luke 8:3 NAB). In the Acts of the Apostles we read of Tabitha, a woman "full of good works and acts of charity" (Acts 9:36), who returns to life through Peter's prayers. We even see the evidence of Tabitha's charity in the mourning women who show Peter the clothes she had made for the impoverished widows of the community. Paul speaks of Phoebe, a deaconess, who "has been a helper of many and of myself as well" (Rom. 16:2). And in describing the character of a Christian woman, he says, " ... she must be well attested for her good deeds, as one who has brought up children, shown hospitality, washed the feet of the saints, relieved the afflicted, and devoted herself to doing good in every way" (1 Tim. 5:10).

"A helper of many." "Full of good works and acts of charity." "One who has brought up children, shown hospitality, washed the feet of the saints, relieved the afflicted." These were the gifts that women brought to the life of the early Christian communities, and they are gifts called for in the role of a Christian wife.

This ability to support life is an innate part of women's character. We can even see it biologically, in the way a woman supports the life of her child during pregnancy and infancy. That is the whole beauty of God's roles for husband and wife: they are perfectly designed for who we are, for our particular abilities and characteristics as men and women.

A woman who sets out to learn more about this role God has designed for her may be surprised at how much it involves. It is often claimed that the role of helper restricts women, that they cannot use all their natural gifts. But in God's eyes, a helper is above all a *useful* person. He will draw on every gift she has—all her potential and all her abilities. In the end, she will probably have trouble finding enough time to fit everything in.

Take a look, for example, at the "perfect wife" described in Proverbs (31:10-31). She does more work than any actual person—male or female—could begin to keep up with. And it's not just housecleaning, either. She rules a large and busy household, with a considerable work force of servants. She feeds and clothes this household, organizes their work, teaches them, and maintains the order of their life. She herself works hard, then sells her produce and invests the money. She is a strong, competent woman, who can work without tiring, take initiative and govern effectively.

Not every Christian woman has to be a "perfect wife." This was probably written as an idealized description, something of a super-wife, and not as a portrait of an actual woman. But it does show that supporting life in the home need not be an unimportant or restricting occupation. A modern wife's actual duties may differ in many ways from those described in Proverbs—for one thing, how many women have a large force of servants to direct?—but that strength, competence, initiative, and wisdom can be hers.

What is all this going to mean practically? What does it mean to support life in a twentieth century family? This is a question that Christian women need to face seriously. They should look for the role that God has for them in the midst of our changing social system. What I will share in the rest of this chapter is wisdom developed by women I know who have been trying to better understand their role as Christian wives.

Support

One purpose of Christian marriage is for husband and wife to help each other become stronger and more mature as individuals. The husband does this for his wife through his leadership and personal care. She in turn is called to support her husband in his life and responsibilities.

A wife is in a unique position to help her husband grow as a man of God. She sees more closely than anyone both his strengths and his failings; she is able to support and affirm God's action within him. Yet a wife needs to learn how to support her husband without taking over his authority in the family. She may be tempted to try to mold her husband, but God has not given her that responsibility. He wants a wife to learn how to support what he is doing in her husband without trying to direct it.

The particular form of support I want to concentrate on here is what I sometimes call "speaking the truth." Very simply, that means pointing out to a person the Christian truth about a particular situation. For a wife, it might mean encouraging her husband during difficulties by reminding him of God's faithfulness. Or it might mean pointing out when his behavior is wrong. Speaking the truth is not the only form of personal support a wife can offer her husband; it is not necessarily even the most important. But it can be the most difficult to master. The very closeness of marriage makes a husband extremely vulnerable to criticism from his wife; she must be able to speak to him in a way that will really support rather than attack him.

Part of this is simply knowing when to speak. The average wife could probably sit down and reel off a whole list of ways her husband should change. Many of her comments would be right on target. But usually that is just what her husband *does not* need to hear. Ordinarily, he needs a lot more appreciation and encouragement from his wife for those things he is doing well. The wife should limit her suggestions for change only to those which are both important and truly helpful. She should ask her husband to tell her which comments he does find helpful, so that she can better learn to judge what she says.

A wife should also offer her views respectfully, recognizing her husband's authority to judge their validity and decide on a response. Respect is vitally important in this area because what starts off as a genuine desire to offer helpful advice sometimes becomes a destructive pattern of critical thoughts and attitudes. Scripture encourages husbands to love their wives and wives to respect their husbands. This may reflect the actual fact that husbands seem more prone to fail in expressing sufficient love for their wives, while wives seem more prone to develop critical attitudes toward their husbands.

Critical attitudes represent a very dangerous problem in married life. I have known women who allowed themselves to indulge in critical, demeaning thoughts about their husbands and then found the habit hard to break even when it was destroying their marriages. Both partners in marriage should guard against any thoughts or attitudes that would choke off their love and respect.

Besides supporting her husband's personal life, a wife is called to help him fulfill the various commitments he has made, both in the home and outside it. In the next section of this chapter, I will discuss ways she can support his commitments within the family; here I want to talk about those outside it, in his work and service. Sometimes a woman will regard commitments outside the home as rivals for her husband's time and attention. She resents the trips out of town that his job requires or evening meetings for Christian service. These feelings often show up in subtle ways. One woman told me that she found herself always bringing up something very important just before her husband had to leave for a meeting. She wasn't even doing this deliberately; it was an almost unconscious way of getting back at him for spending time away from home.

Often a husband does need to pay more attention to his responsibilities in the home. One reason women have learned to resist their husbands' commitments is that our society encourages men to devote themselves so totally to their careers that they must neglect their families. In those circumstances, a wife should talk with her husband and ask him to reconsider his priorities. At the same time, however, it is right that a man be able to function outside the home. Not only does he need to earn a living for the family, but he should be available for Christian service. The Christian people need more men who can take responsible positions of service. This is not a commitment at odds with family life; it is actually a way that the family unit as a whole can serve the Lord through one of its members.

Many of the things a wife can do to support her husband's work and service are really very simple. She can see that dinner is ready in time for him to eat peacefully and still get to his evening meeting. She can have the house in good order, so that the home environment remains peaceful at times when the husband or the whole family is under stress. By doing a good job with her basic responsibilities in the home, she enables her husband to fulfill his commitments.

Beyond that kind of practical support, she should let her husband know she stands behind him in his responsibilities. When he becomes discouraged, when he faces a major decision about his work, when he is called to a more demanding service, he needs to feel that he has his wife with him, that she has faith in him and in his ability to do a good job. That support can make a tremendous difference in his effectiveness as a servant of the Lord.

The last thing I want to say about support is to encourage wives to make room in their lives for their husbands. A wife should try to avoid having each day so full of her own plans and activities that she has no time for things her husband needs to have her do. She should let her husband know that she stands ready as a strong and reliable support to help him in any way she can. There are many small but important ways in which a wife can express personal support for her husband—caring for him when he's sick, greeting him affectionately when he comes home from work, sewing the button back on his shirt. One thing I really appreciate in Anne is her willingness to try to arrange her responsibilities so that she can be with me for the quiet half-hour talk that brings refreshment to a busy day.

Submission

As I mentioned above, a wife is called to help her husband fulfill his commitments within their family. Most importantly, she should support his commitment to be the head of the family, caring for her and preserving the unity of their common life. She can do this by her submission to his authority. The husband's leadership really depends upon her willing submission.

In order to achieve the unity that is the purpose of submission, Scripture makes clear that "wives should submit to their husbands in everything" (Eph. 5:24 NAB). Submission is called for not just when a wife doesn't really care about the decision or when she completely trusts her husband's judgment, but in everything. Selective submission in marriage produces an incomplete unity at best; it still leaves husband and wife as two independent decision makers who must either struggle constantly or settle for the surface peace of separate lives.

It is not always going to be easy for the wife to submit to her husband. A lot of fears can come up about what will happen to her if he is directing things—say, if she gives him charge of her schedule. I know one woman who had an impossible schedule; she had more responsibilities in her home and outside it than she ever had time for. She needed her husband's help to sort out her activities, but she was afraid that if he took charge he would insist she drop some less important activities that she particularly enjoyed. It was hard for her to turn these decisions over to him, but only when she did could he help her put together a workable schedule.

Fears like these often cause even women who out-

wardly accept their husbands' headship to resist full submission. They find ways to "submit" a decision without
actually giving their husbands the freedom to say no. For
example, a wife may make up her mind about what she
wants to do, set up all the plans, and then at the last minute, maybe just before her husband leaves for work, check
with him. "Oh, I forgot to tell you that there's a prayer
meeting tonight I want to go to. I've got everything arranged, and Jane's coming by at 7:30 to pick me up. Is that
alright?" What can he really say at that point?

A woman can also put a lot of emotional pressure on her
husband to get what she wants. She can threaten to be hurt
or to withdraw and act moody. Or she may try the opposite
tactic and soften him up with lots of attention, then try to
slip a question by while he's off guard.

Wives don't necessarily plot out these tactics deliberately. Many times women who snowball or pressure their
husbands believe that they are being perfectly submissive. Nor is this a uniquely feminine trait; plenty of men
under headship use the same tactics. But manipulation has
nothing to do with true submission. It is simply a more
complicated procedure for doing whatever I want.

Another way in which a wife may undermine her husband's authority is by taking the lead in situations which
he ought to direct. Often this appears in small things. One
wife noticed that although her husband officially directed
their family prayers at meals and other times, she always
signalled him when to begin and end. Some women find
that they tend to direct conversations or social situations in
the family, rather than letting their husbands take the lead.
Many times, this kind of dominance by the wife stems
from the husband's failure to take the proper initiative on
his own. But when a wife takes over family leadership for
her husband, she helps to lock him even more firmly into
passivity.

A wife who wants to support her husband's headship must drop any defenses and truly allow him to direct her life. She should bring her problems and concerns to him without waiting until she has settled on her own answers, so that he is able to offer advice and direction. She should submit decisions in such a way that he can freely say yes or no. That includes giving him plenty of time to think about the matter, taking off the emotional pressure, and accepting the final decision with good spirits. If a decision is difficult for her, she can let him know, not by threatening to give him a hard time, but by saying, "This is going to be hard for me. I want to obey you, but I need your support."

Does this mean that a wife has to obey her husband blindly, without voicing her own opinions at all? No. Submission in Christian marriage does involve real obedience, but it also allows plenty of room for the wife to contribute to the decision-making process. The whole point is to strengthen a couple's unity, not to pit his will against hers. A wife actually supports her husband's leadership when she shares her discernment, feelings, and judgment on the questions that affect their life together. Her contribution is vital to his ability to make a wise decision.

A wife should even take a certain initiative to make suggestions to her husband about possible directions for the family or to point out ways that he can improve his exercise of authority. She has to be careful not to undermine him in doing this, but when she offers her suggestions in a real spirit of submission, they can be a valuable aid to her husband. Knowing how his headship is affecting her will help him learn to be a more effective leader.

Above all, I would encourage wives to expect the Lord to work through their husbands' headship. Trust that the Lord will turn even mistakes and poor decisions to the good. One of the biggest obstacles a husband can face in trying to exercise headship is to feel that he always has to be right, that his wife is going to accept his authority only so long as he doesn't make a mistake. A wife should fulfill her responsibility to let her husband know what she thinks about a decision, and then relax and cooperate with him. At times this requires real faith in the Lord, but it is a faith that he will not leave unrewarded.

In fact, any form of submission in Christian life demands trust in God and faith in his plan. The letter to the Ephesians tells us to be "subject to one another out of reverence for Christ" (Eph. 5:21), or as it could be translated, "out of fear of Christ." This verse is sometimes interpreted in the sense of the mutual submission of all Christians one to another. But in the context of Paul's letter, it serves to introduce his instructions regarding authority and submission in specific relationships within the body of Christ, including the relationship of husband and wife. So the passage speaks of these relationships too when it calls us to submit out of reverence for Christ. It is telling us that the submission called for in Christian marriage, or in any relationship within the body of Christ, is not simply someone's good idea. The Lord himself stands behind the governmental structure of his body, the church, and that cell of it which is the family. Thus, wives are told to submit to their husbands "as to the Lord" (Eph. 5:22).

Scripture even calls for submission from the wives of non-Christian husbands, "so that some, though they do not obey the word, may be won over without a word by the behavior of their wives" (1 Pet. 3:1-2). Obviously, the wife of a non-Christian is not required to obey in anything that would involve denying her faith or acting immorally. But the passage does indicate how God rewards the faith of a woman who practices submission out of her reverence for him.

Making a Home

The support given by a Christian wife centers in a special way upon the home. Not that she should never hold a job or perform outside services, but she does have a primary responsibility to care for her family by making the home in which they live.

The role of homemaker deserves careful reconsideration from Christian women. In our modern industrialized society, many homes have lost a great deal of importance. Once the family farm or craftsman's household was a center for work, education, health care, and other vital activities. Today's household, however, is often little more than a place to eat, sleep, and watch television. We go to schools for education, to the office or factory for work, to the supermarket for food, to the hospital for medical care. The home functions mainly as a retreat from the working world, a place for relaxation and rest.

This change particularly affects the wife as the homemaker. She has lost many economic and social functions that were once hers—those described in Proverbs 31, for example. Consequently, many wives, though certainly not all, find themselves dissatisfied with their role in the home. Some reject that role completely. Others fill up their time with shopping or bridge parties or handicrafts. Still others try to make their work more challenging by aiming at the flawless housecleaning, cooking, and interior decorating that they see in women's magazines.

Christianity should offer a different vision for homemaking, a different vision for the home itself. The Christian home ought not to become a refuge from responsibility. It should be a place where God's people can live the life he has called them to—where children can learn the Lord's ways, where the poor and sick receive care, where evangelization goes on, where brothers and sisters find love and support. As the society and institutions around us become more hostile to Christian life and values, it is going to be even more necessary that our homes provide a counter-environment in which that life can still be lived. In the world at large, the home may be losing its importance, but the strength of the Christian home has never mattered more than it does now. And the role of the Christian homemaker has never been more crucial. Wives have a critical responsibility to make the environment in which Christian life can go on.

Because this topic is so important, I encourage wives to discuss with their husbands and with other Christian women how they can make their homes more a place for Christian life. What I have to offer here are a few simple changes a woman can begin to make right away in her approach to homemaking.

The first is to stop thinking of the home as *her* house, and to consider it the place she makes for her husband and children. It is very easy for a wife to start running the home strictly according to her needs and tastes, leaving the husband and children to accommodate themselves to her way of doing things. Some women want the house to look like the magazine pictures, with everything arranged just so. Others don't care how the house looks and make little effort to keep it in order for their families. Either type of home is not really a place designed with the family in mind; it is a place the wife has made for herself, into which the husband and children must somehow fit.

A wife should take stock of everything that goes into the home—the furniture, the cooking, decorating, linens, and so on—and ask herself, "How can I use these things to support my family's life?" A flexible attitude helps—trying new ideas out to see how the home can best be arranged for the life that is lived there. The furniture can be arranged not simply to look nice, but to provide places where people can talk or read or listen to music. Table settings can be used to create a relaxed, warm atmosphere for family meals. If a particularly nice vase is stuck away in the closet, she can get it out and use it to make the house more beautiful. And if there are some things that the family doesn't need for its life together—whether they be all the broken toys the kids never use or the antique sofa that no one can sit on comfortably—she should probably get rid of them. The family only needs possessions that will support what God wants to do in the home.

As she experiments with ways to arrange the house, the wife should be concerned to establish a good order in how things are stored and used. Order in the home contributes a sense of peace and harmony to all the activities that go on there. It is one sign that this is a Christian home. Not that there is some kind of ideal Christian home, which always has fresh flowers on the table and a curtain on every window. But the home of a Christian family should be distinguished by a sense of order, a sense that things are arranged to facilitate the life that goes on there.

To accomplish all this, a wife may not need to spend all her time at home. Women who have a job or other outside commitments can still make a home for their families. We sometimes get the idea that to be a true homemaker, a woman must bake the bread, sew the clothes, can vegetables, refinish furniture, and keep a garden. These are all things some wives may do as part of homemaking, but a woman can also make a home using all the modern services and time-saving conveniences available to her. The important thing is not that she do all the housework single-handed, but that she take a serious responsibility to maintain a place for her family's life.

If her outside activities conflict with that responsibility, she may need to set them aside for a time. When Anne and I began to have children, she found that she wasn't able to handle the babies, run the house, offer hospitality to our many guests, and still provide as much service outside the home as she had. So we decided to cut down on her outside activities while the children were small, so that she could dedicate the necessary time to the complex job she had at home. That has strengthened our family during the last few years. Even if a woman has to make some sacrifices in her career or in the family income in order to give the right attention to her home, she should remember that in God's eyes the life of her family is more important than money, professional status or even Christian service outside the home.

As a woman makes the home a place where God's life can go on, she and her husband can consider ways to open up the home so that it can also support life in the broader Christian community—perhaps by hosting a Bible study or prayer group or by taking in guests and people whom they can serve in the home. A well-ordered Christian home can be a real haven for our brothers and sisters, a place where they too can come to find and live the Lord's life.

The Character of a Christian Wife

Above all else, a Christian wife must be a woman of God. Her strength as a Christian woman is an essential part of the support she gives her husband. Scripture describes many of the qualities that should characterize a Christian woman, and I want to talk about four which are particularly important for wives.

The first is *faith*. The women mentioned in Scripture were all distinguished by a deep faith in the Lord and in his promises to them and their families. They trusted in him whenever troubles came; they had confidence that his word would finally triumph. Sarah, Hannah, Judith, Esther, and Mary were among these "holy women who hoped in God" (1 Pet. 3:5). What Elizabeth said of Mary could be said of them all: "Blessed is she who believed that the promise made her by the Lord would be fulfilled" (Luke 1:45 *Jerusalem Bible*). Indeed, the letter to the Hebrews speaks of Sarah in almost identical terms: " ... she believed that he who had made the promise would be faithful to it" (Heb. 11:11 *Jerusalem Bible*).

In contrast, women in our culture are often prone to fear

and insecurity, to worries about their children, their husbands, the future. Not that they don't have plenty to worry about. The cost of food keeps going up, violence is mounting in the schools, marriages are falling apart—the future is full of threatening uncertainties. But God wants women who can face the future without fear, like the wife of Proverbs who "laughs at the time to come" (Prov. 31:25).

The only way anyone can even read the newspapers without fear these days is to have faith in the Lord. The faith of Christian women should be the same abiding trust in God that characterized the women of the Bible. They too should hold God's promises in their hearts and believe that they will be fulfilled.

A woman of God is also a woman of *love*. Not only is she warm and affectionate toward family and others, but she has an active, loving concern for the needs of God's people. I have already discussed the way Scripture praises women especially for their good deeds of charity, hospitality, and service. That devotion to "doing good in every way" (1 Tim. 5:10) is characteristic of a Christian woman. It shows up in the way she cares for her family. We see it in the home she makes, the food she prepares, the attention she gives her children. Love distinguishes women's service in the Christian community as well, where they have a special responsibility to relieve the afflicted and wash the feet of the saints (see 1 Tim. 5:10).

The third characteristic I want to speak about is what Scripture calls a *quiet spirit*. The first letter of Peter calls this an "imperishable jewel ... which in God's sight is very precious" (1 Pet. 3:4). The easiest way to understand what it means to have a quiet spirit is to think of a woman whose life is in order, who has the peace and security of being in the right relationship with the Lord and her husband. She is able to focus on her responsibilities without letting curiosity and anxiety and emotional pressures dictate the way she acts. She does not talk compulsively and so dominate every conversation, but trusts her husband's leadership. Some of the related words Scripture applies here are "temperate," "serious," "sensible," "modest," "submissive."

A woman with a quiet spirit has a deep peace in her life. She is at peace with herself, with God, with her husband and children. She has strength, but it is a strength that is under control, that can be gentle because she knows God's power is working with her to accomplish whatever needs to happen. Her submissiveness does not come from passivity or fear, but from confidence that she is in her God-given place of responsibility and authority in the body of Christ.

Right now in our culture women are being urged to assert themselves very strongly and push hard to get what they want. But the Lord wants women who can wait for his time to see things happen. This is especially important in the Christian family, where the wife has to be able to resist the urge to take over and instead let the Lord work through her husband's authority.

Finally, a woman of God is distinguished by her *holiness*. Scripture speaks of women who fear God (Judith 8:8) and devote themselves to prayer—"night and day" says Paul (1 Tim. 5:5). It speaks of the reverent behavior by which Christian women should be known (Titus 2:3; 1 Pet. 3:2). A Christian woman's personal relationship to the Lord is an important part of her character and life.

Developing the character of a Christian woman may look like the hardest part of being a wife. Not many women really believe that they can be holy and faith-filled and strong. Often they accept the cultural image of women as weak and vacillating. But I want to say to wives what I said to husbands: this is the person God created you to be. He has given you the gifts and strengths to be a woman of his. As you accept his gifts and his call to you, as you live out the role he has designed for you, the "hidden person of the heart" (1 Pet. 3:4) will be more and more apparent.

The Lord has also given you supports to help you grow and mature as a Christian woman and wife. He offers you a relationship with himself, so that he can teach you through his Word and give you strength through his Spirit. He offers you support through your husband, particularly through the headship your husband can give. Talk to your husband about the kind of woman you want to become; accept the care and direction he can offer you. The Lord also offers the support of other Christian women, who can strengthen you by sharing their encouragement, wisdom and experience. Look for opportunities to build strong sisterly relationships with women who are living the life you have been called to.

Understanding our roles as husbands and wives is fundamental to family life. The marriage relationship remains the heart of the family even after children are born. But when a husband and wife do have children, God begins to show them a new part of his plan. In the next chapters, I want to move on from the discussion of marriage to take a closer look at our life as parents.

Part Two

Parents and Children

CHAPTER ELEVEN

WHO'S IN CHARGE?

I suppose it all started when God said, "Increase and multiply." Once the first parents had their first children, they must have discovered that raising children involves a lot more than multiplication. "What do we do now?" one can picture Adam asking Eve. "Cain and Abel just don't seem to get along."

Happily for everyone, God did not leave matters at "Increase and multiply." Glad as he is when parents bring forth new life, he is equally concerned that children be properly raised. Through the ages, he has guided his people into a great deal of wisdom about childrearing, wisdom preserved for us in the Scriptures. Today when a family begins to increase and multiply, the parents have a resource at hand to help them discover the Lord's wisdom for raising their children.

The current flood of secular childrearing instructions rarely mentions Scripture as a source of wisdom. We hear all about Dr. Spock's opinions, and Dr. Turtle's and Dr. Gordon's, but we rarely hear what God has said through the Scriptures. Yet while the doctors may offer a great deal of sound advice, the basic principles we adopt as Christian parents should be those found in God's Word. Often we need to know something about the culture and times in which Scripture's instructions were written before we can properly understand their meaning. We should always bear in mind, however, that what we are trying to understand is God's word to us, not simply another opinion on the subject.

For the last several years, a number of Christian families in my city have been examining Scripture's instructions on raising children. We have tried to see what they mean today, in light of contemporary social trends, new findings about child development, and our own practical experience as parents. As we have sought to understand and apply these principles, we have found marked changes occurring in our families. Not that all the children have suddenly adopted angelic behavior, but on the whole they have become more peaceful, more cooperative, and happier with themselves and others. We have also seen more of our children open their own lives to the Lord and develop personal relationships with him.

We are not the only ones to notice the change. Other parents, teachers, coaches, sometimes even other children, remark from time to time on the positive differences they see in children who are raised according to biblical principles in a supportive Christian environment.

I do not mean to say that we have all the answers when it comes to raising children. Like all parents, we face difficult situations when we have to puzzle out what to do. But I do feel that we have acquired a workable understanding of the basic scriptural principles for the parent-child relationship. As we have applied these principles, with the guidance of the Holy Spirit and the wisdom gained through trial and error, we have witnessed their good effect on our families.

The next five chapters describe these principles and discuss how parents can apply them in dealing with their children. I will not be able to discuss every problem parents may encounter or how to deal with every age group or social environment. Rather, I want to offer principles that serve as a foundation for the relationship between parents and children. That foundation can then provide the basis for parents' response to individual situations that arise in actual practice.[1]

The Basic Goal

The letter to the Ephesians tells fathers to bring up their children "in the discipline and instruction of the Lord" (Eph. 6:4). That phrase capsulizes the scriptural goal of childrearing: parents have a responsibility to train and instruct their children for the Lord. They are not free to do whatever they want with the children; they must diligently seek out God's purpose for them and raise them according to it. Their primary goal is to raise children who know the Lord and follow his ways.

The responsibility for raising children in the Lord rests in a special way upon the father, as we see from the fact that Paul addresses his instruction in Ephesians to fathers. As head of the family, the father must be particularly concerned for what happens with his children. However, both the Old and New Testaments also make clear that the mother shares that responsibility and the authority that goes with it.

The seriousness with which God views this responsibility is illustrated in the Old Testament story of the high priest Eli (1 Sam. 2:12-4:18). The sons of Eli, who lacked respect for the Lord and his people, abused their position as priests. Eli told them to change their ways, but they paid no attention. Their sinful behavior continued. God

---

1. A number of Christian books discuss the principles of raising children in greater detail than I can attempt here. Among the books I would recommend to parents are Dr. James Dobson's *Dare to Discipline* (Tyndale: 1970) and *Hide or Seek* (Revell: 1974), Richard Strauss's *Confident Children and How They Grow* (Tyndale: 1975), and Jay Kesler's *Let's Succeed with Our Teenagers* (David Cook Publishing: 1973). I would not recommend everything in every one of these books, but they do offer helpful advice from a Christian perspective.

then sent warning to Eli that his entire house would be punished, for "he knew ... his sons were blaspheming God, and he did not restrain them" (3:13). Soon after, both Eli and his sons were dead.

The interesting point here is that Eli had tried to restrain his sons, or at least we would think he had. He told them they were sinning and warned them of the consequences. God apparently expected more vigorous action from this father. It was not enough that he simply correct his sons once; God wanted him to step in and set them right.

Training children for the Lord involves much more than an occasional rebuke or correction. Recently a young man who had grown up in a devout Christian family yet rejected the gospel for many years told me that he probably would have become a Christian as a child if his parents had stopped him from pursuing certain friendships. "The kind of guys I hung around with," he said, "made it impossible to be a Christian." God wants parents to take an active role in ensuring that their children learn his ways. The children's future depends on it, and to some degree, the parents' does too.

As Christian parents, we must see that God has given us a responsibility to take a vigorous role in raising our children. In accepting this responsibility, we must also decide to accept the authority over our children that comes with it. We must decide that we are going to take charge of our children's lives and give them guidance and direction.

People sometimes associate the use of authority with stern, abusive parents, who beat their children instead of showing them love. I explained in an earlier chapter how the patterns of authority taught in Scripture differ from those we usually see practiced in the world. The differences extend to the parent-child relationship. Scripture directs parents to provide authoritative guidance for their children, but at the same time it cautions them against any misuses of their position.

When Scripture tells children to "obey your parents in the Lord," it also tells fathers, "Do not provoke your children to anger" (Eph. 6:1-4). When it says, "Children, obey your parents in everything, for this pleases the Lord," it also says, "Fathers, do not provoke your children lest they become discouraged" (Col. 3:20-21). The authority given to parents is clear; the complete obedience expected of children is clear. But it is also clear that parents are not to use that authority to relieve their own frustrations, cover up their laziness and mistakes, protect their self-esteem, or excuse their failures to listen.

A model for the use of authority between parents and children is provided by Jesus in his relationship with his disciples. He clearly had charge of his disciples. He was their teacher. He corrected them; he admonished and chastised them. But he acted lovingly, patiently, with a long-range view of how the disciples were developing. Parents may find it helpful to bear in mind that one aspect of their authority over their children is a charge from God to form them as disciples.

At the time I first realized that God expected me, as a parent, to take charge of my children, I began to notice that the ones who were actually directing some parts of my family's life were the children—my two-year-old daughter and four-year-old son. They were making decisions about what the family did. They were, to some extent, leading my wife and me.

I know that my home was not alone in that. Many homes today, especially in the United States, are to some degree run by children. Parents often seem incapable of resisting the emotional manipulation that children use so well. The children decide what the family will eat, and how they will spend their time, and what they will do with their money. I believe that the Lord wants Christian parents to become aware of this situation and recognize that they, and not their children, are supposed to provide the direction and leadership in their families.

I want to add here that parents need to use a certain amount of discretion when they actually begin to exercise their authority. A great deal depends on the age of the children involved and the relationship already established between them and the parents. It is usually not too difficult to introduce new principles while children are still very young. With older children, however, who are already used to one pattern of authority in dealing with their parents, making changes can be much more complicated.

A good period of careful preparation should precede any changes in parents' use of discipline and authority, especially if the changes will involve older children. Before the parents do anything, they should take plenty of time together to pray and discuss the new direction. They need some kind of step-by-step strategy for implementing their decisions with each child and in the family as a whole. They should then carefully explain to the children what the changes are and why they are being made.

Sometimes another basic change in the family has to take place before the parents try to exercise more authority. Such a change might involve their own relationship as husband and wife. Or they may need to improve the way they communicate with their children and express affection in the home. This is especially important when there has been a long-standing pattern of neglect or abuse of the children.

In some families, the children have already reached an age and frame of mind that takes them out of the sphere of their parents' authority. This can be true even when they still live at home. In those situations, the parents must make some basic decisions about what they can reasonably expect to see happen in terms of their authority. Although their responsibility as parents remains, it may be impossible to do anything about it except pray and give the children lots of love. Prayer and love have brought many children to the Lord when authority could no longer be used.

When parents do start to take charge of their children, they may find some resistance coming from outside the family. In many ways, the use of parental authority runs counter to the trend of modern culture. More and more childrearing experts and child advocacy groups tell parents to give up any effort to train or instruct their children. Parents are warned to leave children completely free to form their own beliefs and moral values. One widely distributed "bill of rights" for children includes such provisions as a "right" to be free from "religious indoctrination," meaning that parents could be restricted in teaching their children religious beliefs.

The fundamental error in that position is its assumption that all beliefs and values are relative, that no one can claim to know or speak the truth. For Christians, that assumption is totally unacceptable. We know that God is real, that he has revealed himself to us. He has taught us his ways and his laws for our life on earth. He has also taught us the consequence of disobeying his laws—confusion, pain, darkness, and, ultimately, death. When he gives us children, he wants us to teach them to know and follow his ways. It is not a matter of our imposing beliefs on our children, but of instructing them in a truth vital to their own well-being.

No parent will allow a small child to run out into the street without looking for cars. No parent will let a child grow up thinking that two plus two equals five. Parents teach their children the difference between up and down; they teach them not to play with sharp knives; they teach them to talk correctly. And no one suggests that parents are imposing their own concepts or indoctrinating children in their personal beliefs when they insist that they learn these things. Everyone knows that children must learn certain concepts and skills in order to cope with everyday life.

Well, sin is no less real than two plus two equals four. Disobedience to God's laws has consequences just as serious as playing in traffic. Children need to know the ways of God every bit as much as they need to know arithmetic or reading. Quite frankly, the knowledge of God's law is far more important to a child's future peace and happiness than anything else he can learn.

Once when I was sharing these ideas with a group of parents, an obviously excited father jumped to his feet. "I see it," he said. "I'm spending all my time and effort teaching my children to read and add and cross the street, but I'm not taking time to teach them the laws of God that are really more important. I've been duped. I've swallowed a lie."

I believe God wants to lead all Christian parents to that same insight. If parents do not take an active, vigorous role in forming and teaching their children, other forces will. It is not as if children grow up in a vacuum where no one besides their parents can teach them beliefs and values. If we turn on the television, or pick up a magazine, or listen to a record, we can learn lots of values and moral judgments. If we could go to school with our children, we would see how much the values of their friends and the beliefs of their teachers affect them. Yet how often do the values that children learn from television and radio and the latest fad among their friends conform to God's word? Parents who fail to take an active role in forming their children are handing them over to be formed by the world, the flesh, and the devil.

In fact, the cultural forces shaping our children have become so strong that even when parents do try to train their children, their efforts seem relatively weak. Television advertising backed by millions of dollars is far more sophisticated in influencing children than anything an isolated Christian family can do. Christian parents should not try to struggle through entirely on their own. It is more important than ever that they band together with other Christians around them to form an environment for their children that can counteract the secular environment. This will be discussed further in another chapter.

CHAPTER TWELVE

THE GOAL OF TRAINING

If parents do take an authoritative role in training and forming their children, what goal should they work toward? What kind of people do they want their children to become as they grow up? What values and patterns of behavior do they want them to learn? Parents need a clear vision for their children before they can begin to train them.

Training Children to Love the Lord

First of all, Christian parents should aim at raising children who love and serve the Lord. This is perhaps their most important goal. They should tell their children about the Lord and teach them about his love, so that they come to know the Lord personally.

Few Christians need to be told that they should want to bring up children who love the Lord. Wherever I go to talk about family life, parents ask what they can do to tell their children about God. Often, these parents feel baffled because their efforts run up against indifference or resistance in the children. Their children don't want to go to church. They don't want to hear about the Lord. They don't want any part in family devotions. It is easy for parents to lose faith and decide that their children really don't have any desire for the Lord or his life.

A child's crust of indifference to God can seem impenetrable, but in the final analysis it is only a crust. Every child has been created by and for God; as St. Augustine said, "Our hearts are restless until they rest in You." But the environment surrounding children in their schools and among their friends leaves them little room to develop that relationship with God. Our culture does a very effective job of isolating children and adults in two separate worlds; if children do not see peers who are interested in the Lord (and they usually don't), they can easily decide that Christianity is only for adults. It takes a special effort for parents to break down that barrier and show their children that the Lord's love includes them too.

At one point, the group of Christians I was part of in Michigan realized that most of our children were not personally involved in our life with the Lord. One man had a conversation with a group of our kids in their "pre-teen" years. As they talked about prayer and having a relationship with Jesus, child after child said, "Gee, I didn't know we could do that." "I didn't know that I should sing out and praise God." "I didn't know that kids could raise their hands to pray." "I thought all that was just for adults."

These were children who had seen people praying, had heard people tell about God's love, had watched even their own parents change through the power of the Holy Spirit. Yet the idea that they could share in all this came as a real revelation for many of them. Since then, we have made greater effort to draw our children into our life, and we have seen much fruit come of it.

Scripture speaks clearly of God's desire that children share their parents' spiritual life. After the exodus, Moses commanded the Israelites to remember God's deeds and teach them to their children, so that each new generation could share in everything God had done for their parents. In the same way, the Lord wants Christian children included in all that their parents experience of his life. He does not want to have to start all over again teaching every generation the same lessons. He wants to build children's lives upon the foundation he has established in their parents' lives.

Later in this chapter, I will discuss what parents can do to teach their children about the Lord and about the other things children need to learn. But I would like to add one caution here. While the desire for God is present in children's hearts, the resistances they feel toward hearing about the Lord can also be very real. Maybe it comes from the influence of other children or of teachers; maybe it is due to shyness about discussing the Lord with adults. Or maybe it reflects problems between the child and the parents. A child who resents or fears his parents' erratic behavior or lack of affection will not be open to what they say about God.

Parents need not get discouraged when they meet resistance to the Lord in their children, but they should not ignore it either. It takes more than a mechanical application of biblical principles to bring a child to the Lord. They should draw on the discernment that God will give them and on the wisdom of more experienced Christian parents to find the right way to help each child over these obstacles.

I know a couple who reconverted to Christianity at a time when some of their children were already teenagers. All of the children eventually became Christians, but the experience was different for each child. Parental authority proved to be a key for the oldest son. He dragged his heels about going to a prayer meeting until the night his parents said, "You are going with us," and took him. He gave his life to the Lord at that meeting. With another son, however, the parents did little more than provide an atmosphere in which the Lord could work personally. As he told them later, "I was lying in bed one night practicing what I would say if I were going to give my life to the Lord. I guess he didn't consider it a rehearsal."

In the final analysis, it is always the Lord himself who must draw our children into a relationship with him. Our effort, skill, and techniques will not suffice alone. We should expect the Lord to work within our children and to give us the insight and wisdom we need to help them along. Sometimes the most important thing a parent can do for a particular child is simply to pray regularly for that child. There are points at which our words lose their effectiveness, when God must work directly in a child's heart.

Training Children to Love Their Fellow Christians

As they learn to love God, children must also learn to love other Christians as their brothers and sisters. In chapter three, I mentioned how important it is for a married couple to relate as brother and sister in the Lord. But I also explained that none of Scripture's instructions on how to relate as Christian brethren are directed exclusively to married couples. They are principles of conduct for all Christians, including children.

Scripture says so much about how brothers and sisters in Christ should treat each other that I can only mention some of the most important points here. Scripture stresses the whole concept of committed love, so different from the romanticized version of love popularized in songs and movies. It provides principles of repentance and forgiveness for restoring relationships broken by misunderstanding or wrongdoing. Scripture also teaches Christians how to speak to one another, how to handle disagreements, how to express love and support, how to care for one another's material needs. These are all important lessons for Christian life, and lessons which children can learn.

For example, I know many parents who make a practice of teaching their children how to repent for wrongdoing and how to forgive one another. When the kids fight or get angry, their parents not only correct them, they also encourage them to repent, forgive, and be reconciled. The children learn that they can settle their disputes in love and go back to playing together, rather than hang on to grudges that stand between them for days or years.

In one family, the parents set out to teach their children the right ways to speak to each other. The kids had been constantly teasing, mocking one another, and putting each other down. Their parents found a few passages from Scripture about speech, including a proverb that says, "Some people like to make cutting remarks, but the words of the wise soothe and heal" (Prov. 12:18 *Living Bible*). They posted the passages in the house, and whenever they had to correct their children for saying something unkind, they referred back to them. After several months, the way the children talked to one another began to change. By the end of a year much of the previous arguing had disappeared.

Children should also learn to show respect and honor for other people. Scripture speaks often of showing honor to "all men" (1 Pet. 2:17), especially to those in positions of authority. We are told to "Pay ... respect to whom respect is due, honor to whom honor is due" (Rom. 13:7). A wife is to "see that she respects her husband" (Eph. 5:33); slaves are to "regard their masters as worthy of all honor" (1 Tim. 6:1), advice that would also apply to employees and their employers. Yet a common characteristic of modern society is a lack of respect, even for those Scripture tells us to respect the most.

A key element in teaching children to show proper respect and honor is their relationship with their parents. Scripture places special emphasis on the respect due to parents. It even holds a place among the ten commandments: "Honor your father and mother." Indeed, as Paul notes in the letter to the Ephesians (6:2), this is the first commandment to carry a promise: "... that your days may be prolonged, and that it may go well with you, in the land which the Lord your God gives you" (Deut. 5:16).

The book of Sirach (3:2-6, 12-14 NAB) spells out more completely what this commandment means:

> For the Lord sets a father in honor over his children; a mother's authority he confirms over her sons. He who honors his father atones for sins; he stores up riches who reveres his mother. He who honors his father is gladdened by children, and when he prays he is heard. He who reveres his father will live a long life; he obeys the Lord who brings comfort to his mother ... My son, take care of your father when he is old; grieve him not as long as he lives. Even if his mind fail, be considerate with him; revile him not in the fullness of your strength. For kindness to a father will not be forgotten, it will serve as a sin offering—it will take lasting root.

Most parents should consider whether they show the proper respect for their own parents and for the legitimate authorities in their church and government. At times the way we express respect for human authorities will be limited by our commitment to obey the Lord; Jesus himself warned that obedience to his word would sometimes conflict with obedience to earthly authorities. But normally, respect and honor for those in authority, especially parents, is the pattern we should follow ourselves and teach to our children.

Service is another important lesson that children need to learn. In general, modern society tries to preserve children from responsibility, with many bad consequences. Some sociologists trace the frustration and rebellion characterizing modern adolescents back to their isolation from responsibility. Christian children should learn that they do have a responsibility toward others, that their time is not their own, but is really at the call of their brothers and sisters. Many families I know are trying to give their children responsible work at home so that they can learn to serve and be useful to their brethren. The children are not paid for their work in the house: it is considered a part of their responsibilities. Those children receive allowances as a part of their share in the family's resources, not as a reward for their work.

These are all lessons which many Christians have had to struggle to learn as adults. We grew up learning certain attitudes from the society around us—to hold grudges, to deny guilt, to put others down, to work only for our own profit. It was hard to learn to forgive, to accept responsibility for our own wrongdoing, to build up our brothers and sisters, to serve others unselfishly. The Lord does not want our children to have to repeat all our struggles to change these behavior patterns. He wants them to learn how to act toward their brothers and sisters now, while they are growing up. Then, when they leave our homes, they will leave as mature Christians, ready to take their places among God's people in love and service.

Training Children to Deal with Secular Life

Children must also learn how to relate to the world around them. Basically, that means learning the practical skills they will need in daily life—everything from brushing their teeth to driving a car. I remember having to teach my children how to brush their teeth. For a long time, my wife or I always did the brushing for them. But one day, we began wondering why as they were getting older they weren't able to brush their teeth themselves. We realized that we had never taught them how. We actually had to say, "Now kids, you hold your toothbrush like this, and you move it up and down" and so on. It seemed such a simple thing, but we realized that even in the simplest matters we had to teach our children if they were to learn the skills they need.

As children get older, teaching them practical skills can also involve equipping them to work and earn a living. Many children today grow up in almost total ignorance of the ordinary working world that will be so much a part of their adult lives. Their parents can help to prepare their children for the future by educating them about the value of work and helping them understand what "going to work" means. One man I know, an accountant, regularly brings his children into the office to help out, so that they can see how a business office functions. Another father who works as a salesman occasionally takes his son with him on his rounds, so that the boy can see his father at work.

In training children in the various skills they will need as adults, parents should keep a careful watch on their own motives and attitudes. It is not necessary for every child to go to college or get a white-collar job. Christian parents should not subject their children to the kind of pressure to succeed that the world imposes. They should help each child discover the way he or she is best suited to contribute to the Christian community. Among Christians, there should be a real sense of helping each member of the body find the proper place, even in secular employment.

Besides learning these necessary practical skills, Christian children must learn how to maintain Christian beliefs and standards in a world that is becoming ever more pagan. Jesus told his disciples that while they were not to withdraw from the world, they were not to identify with it either (see John 17:15). Children are going to need some help figuring out what that means for them. They need to know how to respond to the values and attitudes confronting them on television. They need to know how to respond to abuse from people who do not live by Christian standards. They need to learn compassion for the poor, the oppressed, and others who are trodden down by the world's selfishness.

For children in America especially, simply going to school everyday often means entering a hostile and challenging environment in which they must learn to stand by their Christian values. Many parents find it helpful to talk a little with their children each day after school, so that they can find out what has happened that day and help the kids understand any difficulties that have come up. One family had taught their children to be friendly and outgoing, showing real Christian love for others. But when their fourteen-year-old son started going to a new junior high school, he tried smiling at some students in the hall and got roughed up in return. His parents had to explain how he could be friendly without asking for trouble.

Some other parents face even more challenging situations, where the school environment actually threatens their children's views and attitudes as Christians. The pressures on children to conform to their peers is tremendous, usually much worse than anything their parents face among adults. Parents must take every opportunity to teach their children how to deal with these pressures and how to understand the situation they are in. Difficult as this is, it can help children develop the strength they will need to be witnesses to Christ in an unbelieving world.

CHAPTER THIRTEEN

THE MEANS OF TRAINING

Training children for the Lord encompasses so much that parents may feel a little discouraged. "Where do we begin? How can I possibly train my children in all these things when I have such a hard time getting them to clean their rooms?"

It does take a lot of effort to raise children according to scriptural principles. And we may have good grounds for doubting our ability to do it. Yet the fact remains that as Christian parents we have no other real option. We are like the apostles, who had to say, even when Jesus' words seemed impossible, "Where else can we go, Lord? You alone have the words that bring life" (see John 6:68).

As we consider the elements that go into raising children, however, we should bear in mind that God did not intend isolated Christian couples to carry this responsibility alone. He himself offers to be our helper, giving us strength and wisdom directly through a personal relationship with him. He also wants us to unite with other Christians, so that we can share the task of raising children by helping and encouraging one another, sharing our wisdom and strength.

Three elements go into the actual training of children: example, teaching, and discipline. No single one of these can be fully effective in isolation from the other two. Discipline helps to reinforce example and teaching, but without them it is self-defeating. Imagine the results if a mother tried to teach her daughter sewing not by showing her how, but by punishing her each time she made a mistake. The daughter might never even learn how to thread a needle, but she would build up plenty of frustration and resentment.

In this chapter, I want to discuss the first two elements—example and teaching. The next two chapters will focus on discipline. But before I begin, I want to discuss one key factor for making any element of training children work—the unity of the mother and father.

I have already talked quite a bit about the importance of unity for what God wants to accomplish through a married couple. Perhaps nowhere can that be seen so clearly as in the raising of children. The gifts that God gives a couple as mother and as father are not identical: they are designed to complement one another. Parents must use their complementary gifts together, in unity, in order to give their children what they need.

Unity between the parents is also important in terms of the effect it has on the training of children. When my son John was learning to dress himself, Anne worked with him every day, teaching him how to do things on his own. "Now John, put your pants on. Now put your shirt on." But when I helped John get dressed, I would do it all myself, because it took about five times longer to show him what to do. The next time Anne tried to get John to dress himself, he wouldn't cooperate. I suppose he figured that I would do it for him later.

Once Anne and I saw what was happening, we recognized that our lack of unity on this one point was undermining the teaching our child needed. While this was only a minor incident, it showed us the implications that disunity between us would have on larger matters.

It is important, then, that parents approach the training of their children together. They need to spend time discussing what is going on with each child—what that child needs to learn and how they can teach her or him. When they agree on some approach, they should also agree to support and reinforce one another. Their children should know that mother and father are united in their approach to raising them.

Example

No parent can teach children about a way of life that he or she is not actually living. Children see their parents very close up, and are greatly influenced by what they see. If their parents' behavior does not square with the ideas the parents teach, the children will not take those ideas seriously.

Few parents realize how much their example teaches their children. One man was shocked to hear his child repeat some critical remarks he had made about a Christian friend. He wanted to teach his children the right way to speak about other people, but his own behavior was teaching them something different. That is just the kind of behavior that does teach children how to act. They learn a lot from small things like what dad says when he hits his thumb with a hammer or how mom reacts when another car cuts her off in traffic.

At one point, Anne and I decided to teach our children some basic table manners, especially teaching them to say "Please" and "Thank you" when asking for things. Several weeks of uneven progress went by. Then one of the kids asked, "How come adults don't have to say 'Please' and 'Thank you'?" We realized that we were not using the same manners that we wanted them to learn. Naturally, that was creating some confusion. If we wanted to teach our children even a simple thing like saying "Please" when asking for mashed potatoes, we had to start by giving them the right example.

Children also learn from larger things. They know when trouble hits the family—when daddy loses his job or Aunt Sally dies or mom is sick—and they watch to see how their parents respond to the crisis. If they see them respond with fear, they learn fear. If they see them get depressed, they learn depression. Sometimes if they see their parents respond badly, they react in the opposite direction, perhaps by stifling their emotional responses. If they see them react with confidence in God, they learn faith. One way or another, they are formed and taught by the way their parents act.

All this is even more true in training children as Christians. Christianity is more than a set of doctrines, which children can learn by rote. It is also a way of life, which they must see in practice. Everyone hears about kids who were raised by extremely devout parents, but turned out to be the worst lot in town. Once I asked the director of an evangelistic ministry why there are so many of these stories, especially about ministers' children. Both this director and his wife are the children of ministers who were themselves children of ministers, and I thought they might have some insight.

He answered, "When I hear about ministers' children who don't turn out well, I often find that their parents have been only grudgingly fulfilling their responsibilities as Christians. Maybe dad preaches a sermon on Sunday, but when he comes home he gripes about the congregation. The parents grumble and complain about their duties— 'Darn it, I've got to go to a board meeting' or 'Oh no, I've got to go talk to the Smiths.' And their children really get two signals: one, that you should be a Christian, but secondly, that Christianity is a drag."

The wife added that her parents and grandparents had loved the Lord and loved serving the Lord. They rejoiced when they were transferred out to the missions, rejoiced when they had to suffer hardships in their service, and rejoiced when they had to work long hours. They were glad to give their lives to the Lord and they communicated that joy and excitement to their children. She had learned from her parents not just doctrinal beliefs, but a whole spirit of Christian living.

Other Christian families find this same principle true in raising their children. One couple tells of the day their two-and-a-half year old son started to fall down the stairs. As he grabbed for the railing to save himself, he yelled, "Jesus, help me!" The parents had never explicitly taught their son to ask Jesus for help when he was in danger, but he had seen them call on the Lord for help in their troubles and so he did the same.

Another woman describes the way her children were affected by seeing their parents take time each day for personal prayer. The children could see how much daily prayer meant to their parents, and became curious about it. One of the little boys got so interested in daddy's prayer time that he would peek in the door to watch. Soon, the children asked if they could take a prayer time each day, and the parents were able to start teaching them how to pray.

Because example does play a critical role in training children, it is vital that parents submit themselves fully to the Lord, letting him train and teach them as they try to train their children. When children see in their parents the good effect of following the Lord, they will be attracted to him, too.

There is a lesson here for parents who avoid involvement with other Christians in their church or in a prayer group because they think that spending every possible moment at home will make them better parents. While some parents who have actually neglected their families do need to pull back from outside activities, on the whole a greater balance is needed in this matter. If parents do not get the fellowship they need with other Christians, if they are not called on to greater devotion and service, if they do not receive teaching and guidance to help their spiritual growth, then they will not really have a great deal to offer their children, no matter how much time they spend with them. Parents who want to raise their children for Christ must begin by living for Christ themselves.

Teaching

Important as it is, example by itself is not a fully effective tool for training children. That may seem a surprising statement after all I have said, but the fact is that children do not get full benefit from their parents' example unless they also learn what that example means and how it applies to them. My children got a wonderful example of faithful tooth-brushing from Anne and me: every night we brushed their teeth. But they never learned how to do it themselves until we actually taught them.

The book of Deuteronomy says some interesting things about instructing children in the Lord's ways and commandments. Moses tells the people of Israel to "drill [these words] into your children. Speak of them at home and abroad, whether you are busy or at rest. Bind them at your wrist as a sign and let them be as a pendant on your forehead. Write them on the doorposts of your houses and on your gates" (Deut. 6:7-9 NAB).

Not only are the people to keep God's word before their children, but they are to explain to them the personal significance of their covenant with the Lord. "Later on, when your son asks you what these ordinances, statutes and decrees mean which the Lord, our God, has enjoined on you,

you shall say to your son, 'We were once slaves of Pharaoh in Egypt, but the Lord brought us out of Egypt with his strong hand . . .' " (Deut. 6:20-21).

The way of life God has taught us is important, and we should be diligent in teaching it to our children. This does not necessarily mean setting up a classroom in the home to have weekly lessons. Often teaching children means nothing more than taking time to explain things they have seen us doing. But even that will not happen automatically. We must make a deliberate effort to explain what we are doing and why, to testify to things God has done for us personally. We can even enlist the home environment to help us teach the Lord's ways—perhaps not in the exact way prescribed in Deuteronomy, but by using Christian music and art to speak of God and his commandments.

I mentioned earlier the children who wanted to take a daily prayer time after watching their parents do so. When those children started trying to pray each day, they did not really know what to do. They would try to pray for fifteen or twenty minutes, and get bored after just a few. When they complained about this, their parents saw that they had to teach their children how to pray.

For instance, the mother sat down with the oldest girl, then twelve. She explained to her: "Take five or ten minutes to praise God and give thanks out loud, then take some time to play on your guitar and sing some Christian songs, then pray a while for specific people and situations." She prayed together with her daughter for a few days, while the girl learned how to use a prayer time. Soon the twelve-year-old was enjoying her prayer life and was growing in a relationship with the Lord.

Besides explaining the parents' example, teaching also gives children the information and perspective they need to form Christian attitudes and values. Christian teaching that is restricted to time spent in a church or in religious education classes rarely proves effective. Teaching must go on all the time, in all the events of life, in order to form a child as a Christian. From a very early age, children see and experience a lot that they do not understand. They see suffering and pain and injustice; they encounter cruelty and rejection from other people; they have to deal with sometimes bewildering feelings about themselves and others.

These things affect children deeply. If they get no guidance from their parents about how to understand and respond to their experiences, they start interpreting them on their own and settling on their own ways of handling things. The conclusions they reach completely on their own are likely to be based on fear or self-concern rather than on the Lord's truth.

It is very important, then, that parents begin teaching their children attitudes and values at an early age. Most of this teaching can happen informally in conversation with children. One of the best ways to begin teaching children is simply to spend time developing good communication with them. One couple I know makes a point of discussing world events or dating or other important topics at dinner, so that their children have a chance to share their thoughts and then to hear their parents' view in terms of Christian truth. Some parents make a point of spending special time with each of their children every week. For example, one father spends an hour on Saturday with one of his two sons, and an hour on Sunday with the other.

Anne and I have found bedtime a particularly good opportunity for talking with our children. Whenever the circumstances permit it, we spend a little time with them after they are ready for bed, talking over the events of the day. When our son John was about five, we discovered that he would talk about his day more freely when we asked, "Did anything make you sad today? Did anything make you happy?" Often nothing of earth-shaking importance emerged—some days all it takes to make a five-year-old happy is riding his tricycle. But at other times those questions helped him to open up and tell us things that were on his mind.

Our oldest daughter, who has a different personality, never responded much to those questions. She reacts to things she doesn't like by getting angry rather than sad. One night she blurted out, "Nothing made me happy or sad today, but something made me mad." Now that question helps us stay in touch with her. It has also given us a chance to teach her how to handle her anger in a positive way.

One evening as I talked with John, he was sad because someone at school would not be his friend. Since there is a Christian way to respond to rejection, I took that opportunity to teach John something about it. He needed to hear that he was lovable: that I loved him, and his mother loved him, and his other friends loved him. He needed to understand that people do sometimes say cruel things to one another, and that while it is painful he shouldn't let it discourage him. He needed to hear that he could forgive the other little boy and be ready to make up with him if the chance came, at the same time being realistic about how people treat each other.

Some childrearing experts encourage parents to listen to their children's problems passively, without offering any advice. The idea is that children will then have to solve their own problems. But if parents want their children to learn how to deal with their problems in the Lord's way, they should not be afraid to teach and advise them.

Parents can also use the time they spend talking with their children to teach basic Christian truths. Even small children often ask questions about life and death and the nature of God. In fact, it is sometimes a challenge to find answers for their questions. "How big is God?" they may ask. "Why do we talk to Jesus when we can't see him?" "How can Jesus be God and man?" "Where is heaven?"

After an initial gulp and a quick prayer for help, a parent can usually find some simple explanation that satisfies childrens' curiosities while helping them toward a knowledge of God.

I have found that my children can understand simple explanations of truths about the Trinity, God's justice, and the resurrection from the dead. And they find a measure of real Christian joy in knowing these things—in knowing, for example, that death has no sting for a Christian. It affects their lives even now by giving them a different perspective on the things that happen each day.

As parents begin to develop good communication with their children and become sensitive to opportunities to teach them, they will find many unexpected opportunities arising. One evening I was sitting on the sofa reading a magazine with two of my children sitting on either side of me. As I turned one page, we came upon a photograph of some starving Asian children. "Gee, who are those people?" the kids asked. "They're little children," I told them, "and they're poor and starving." Of course, the kids wanted to know why children were starving, and soon we were talking about poverty and suffering and injustice, what God wanted to do about it, and what part we as Christians had to play in God's plan.

A woman I know found an opportunity to teach her daughter an important lesson when they went to pick out frames for new glasses. The girl was in her early teens, and her mother gave her a lot of freedom to pick the frames she wanted. She thought her daughter did a good job of choosing frames that were both sturdy and attractive, so she paid for them and prepared to leave. But then she noticed that her daughter seemed unhappy.

"What's the matter, Sharon?" she asked.

It turned out that Sharon didn't think her mother really liked the glasses, because she had not said much about them. When her mother explained that she thought the glasses were fine, everything seemed settled. But on the way home, Sharon became upset again, this time with a girl who was riding in the car with them. Sharon thought her friend was thinking something unpleasant about her, which the girl was not thinking. At that point, Sharon's mother realized what the real problem was: her daughter needed to learn that not everything she felt other people were thinking was true.

Using that as an opportunity to teach her daughter, the woman explained that we can easily be deceived about the thoughts of others—deceived by our own fears or our mis-judgment or even by Satan. She pointed out that Sharon had done the right thing in bringing out what she thought the other person was thinking—that enabled her to find out the truth—but she also pointed out that Sharon needed to become more discerning about her feelings.

To take advantage of such opportunities, parents have to really listen to their children. They must be alert to the inner concerns and feelings that lie behind their words and actions. Very few parents actually take the time to listen to their children, and so miss many chances to help them. In addition, when children feel that their parents do not listen, they usually stop talking to them altogether.

So far, I have mostly discussed informal, on-the-spot teaching. There is also a place for carefully planned teach-ing. In teaching practical skills, for example, parents can-not wait for chance opportunities to arise. If they want their children to learn how to cook or make house repairs, they must work with them over a period of time.

One young man has told me that as he was growing up, his parents often assigned him very complex chores with-out taking much time to teach him how to do them. They would tell him to paint the back fence, give him paint and a brush, but not teach him how to paint. Naturally, he never did a very good job at his chores, and he grew up feeling incompetent about any work he tried.

This man saw a marked contrast to his experience when he lived for a year with a Christian family in which the parents made a special effort to teach their children how to do chores well. They took time to figure out which chores would really be best for each of the children—what would challenge them without exceeding their abilities. They took time to explain why each chore was important, so that the children could see their work as worthwhile. And they took time to teach the children how to do their work. Rather than explain the job only once, they would work with each child for the first few weeks until the child could do the work alone.

It takes parents much longer to teach a child a chore than to go ahead and do the work themselves. But careful training makes a real difference for the children. They do not grow up feeling incompetent in their work; they learn to do chores well and take satisfaction in them.

Planned-out teaching can also be very helpful in dealing with persistent behavioral problems. Here it is especially important that parents work as a united team for their children. They need to talk together about what each child needs to learn and the best way to teach it.

One couple told me they had a very hard time controlling their teenage daughter's diet. Every day she stopped on her way home from school to buy candy and snacks that left her with no appetite for dinner. The parents told her not to stop at the store, but their words had little effect. So they talked together about the problem to decide what they should do next.

Among other things, they felt that they should teach their daughter about her nutritional needs. One reason she had trouble obeying them in this matter was that she did not understand how she could harm herself by eating only candy. So they spent some time with their daughter explaining her body's nutritional needs and the damage that could come from ignoring them. It came as quite a surprise to the girl, and helped give her the desire to overcome her bad eating habits.

The whole concept of teaching one's children—whether informally or more systematically—may seem strange to parents. They think, "I've never studied elementary education" or "I'm not a Sunday school teacher." "I send my kids to school for teaching; that's not my job." But God has given parents a responsibility for teaching their children, a responsibility they should not hand over blindly to others. They do not have to do the whole job—school plays a part, and Sunday school or CCD plays a part, and Scouting or sports or other activities play a part. Yet the most important teaching in a child's life—the teaching that shapes the child's personality and thinking and relationship with God—should come from the parents. Once parents decide to accept that responsibility, they should look to the Lord and to their brothers and sisters in Christ for the help they need to carry it out.

CHAPTER FOURTEEN

THE FUNCTION OF DISCIPLINE

The saying "Spare the rod and spoil the child" has been around so long that we sometimes forget it derives from the Bible. Scripture says quite a bit about spanking children, and often what it says is blunt enough to shock our modern ears. "Thrash [your son's] sides while he is still small," advises the book of Sirach (30:12 NAB). "Beat him with the rod," adds Proverbs (23:14). And those are not the only such passages in the Bible.

I am not quoting these passages to encourage parents to snatch up sticks and go hunting for their smallest children. I only want to point out at the very beginning that Scripture does consider physical discipline an important part of raising children. Today, after all, the very mention of spanking can arouse heated reactions. One friend of mine got a visit from the county welfare department after a neighbor saw him spanking his child and called to report the "child-beating" next door.

The word discipline has many meanings besides spanking; in its broadest sense it encompasses all the training and formation a child receives. In this chapter, however, I want to use the word to speak specifically about chastisement or punishment. Punishment is not the beginning and end of raising children; a spanking won't take the place of the parents' example or of careful, patient teaching. But in the broader context of a child's formation, when both example and teaching are going on, there is a definite place for discipline.

Discipline has a specific role in teaching a child the consequences of not heeding parental instructions. A child who sees no consequences attached to the parent's words feels free to disregard them. Discipline backs up words with clear, immediate consequences.

For example, imagine a little girl whose parents tell her not to hit her baby brother on the head with her toy hammer. If nothing happens when she hits him, she will probably go right on. If she gets spanked, however, she learns that hitting her baby brother has painful consequences—for her.

Not everyone agrees that a spanking or other form of discipline is really the best way to back up parental instruction. Many child-rearing theories advise parents to reason with children instead. One widely read book counsels parents just to tell their children frankly how they feel about undesireable conduct. In the case of a little girl who hits her baby brother, the parents would say something like, "Oh, I get scared when I see you hit your brother! I'm so afraid he is going to get hurt!"

Whether or not this would really convince a little girl to lay off her brother, the whole approach is seriously flawed in terms of raising children as Christians. For one thing, it teaches children to forget any objective concept of right and wrong. They only have to consider the way other people feel about their actions. In this case, there is nothing inherently wrong with pounding on baby brothers; it just happens to frighten mommy and daddy.

In addition, this type of reasoning does not teach children that they will bear the consequences of their own wrongdoing. The little girl in question learns only that hitting her baby brother can affect her parents: they might be scared by it. If she is a bit older, she might even realize that it could affect her brother: he could get his skull cracked. But she would never learn that doing something wrong has consequences for her as well. The notion of God's judgment on sin could come as quite a jolt to her later on.

Scripture speaks quite clearly about the inadequacy of reasoning alone as a means of reinforcing parental instruction. One proverb says: "By mere words a servant is not disciplined, for though he understands, he will not give heed" (Prov. 29:19). Another proverb helps explain why this is so: "Folly is bound up in the heart of a child, but the rod of discipline drives it far from him" (Prov. 22:15). Children do not naturally want to do the right thing all the time. They, too, have to deal with the sinful self-will that Scripture elsewhere calls the flesh. It is not that children are inherently evil, but they are not inherently holy either.

By itself, reasoning cannot break through the inborn folly of human self-will. Children need a vivid experience of the consequences that follow wrongdoing to help them resolve to do right. Discipline provides that experience.

Will It Hurt?

Discipline is painful, of course; it is *supposed* to be painful. The consequences of doing wrong have to be unpleasant enough that children will want to avoid them. Many parents shrink back from disciplining their children because they don't want to inflict pain on them. I remember the first time I spanked my son. He cried, and I thought, "How can I do this to him?" I just couldn't reconcile my love for John with doing anything that made him cry.

But Scripture does not recognize any distinction between loving children and disciplining them. On the contrary, it views discipline as a necessary part of parental love. "He who spares the rod hates his son," says the book of Proverbs, "but he who loves him is diligent to discipline him" (Prov. 13:24). The letter to the Hebrews points out that "for the moment all discipline seems painful rather than pleasant; later it yields the peaceful fruit of righteousness to those who have been trained by it" (Heb. 12:11). Parents discipline their children not because they want to cause them pain, but because they want to give them the peace of a righteous life.

The Bible does recognize the conflicting feelings parents have when they spank their children. When I felt bad about spanking John, I remembered the proverb that says: "Do not withhold discipline from a child; if you beat him with a rod, he will not die. If you beat him with the rod, you will save his life from Sheol" (Prov. 23:13-14). I thought, "Whoever wrote this proverb really knew the concerns I would have. He's telling me I don't have to worry; this isn't going to kill John, this is going to save his life."

Today, I look back with amusement at my early dismay about spanking. But I can also see that we modern parents need to free ourselves of sentimentalizing tendencies that make us reluctant to administer discipline. Hypersensitivity to children's feelings leads many parents into a real emotional bondage, like that described in the book of Sirach: "He who spoils his son will have wounds to bandage, and will quake inwardly at every outcry ... Pamper your child and he will be a terror for you, indulge him and he will bring you grief" (Sir. 30:7-9 NAB). Scripture promises that children can be a joy, but it links that promise to the parent's willingness to discipline: "Discipline your son, and he will give you rest; he will give delight to your heart" (Prov. 29:17).

People sometimes suggest that all this biblical advice

about discipline is just another cultural left-over from ancient Palestine. But the Bible specifically links its words
on discipline to the trans-cultural reality of God's own
love. "For whom the Lord loves he reproves, and he chas-
tises the son he favors" (Prov. 3:12 NAB). The Lord himself uses discipline to correct his people—because he
loves them! This is a lesson which the Old Testament
teaches over and over as it describes God's dealings with
Israel. The letter to the Hebrews, commenting on the
proverb above, adds, "If you are left without discipline, in
which all have participated, then you are illegitimate children and not sons" (Heb. 12:8).

Despite its painfulness, then, discipline can be an expression of love. But to be experienced as love, it must
take place in the context of a loving personal relationship.
The people who most easily experience God's discipline
as a sign of his love are those who have already experienced that love in other ways. Children, too, must have
experienced their parents' love before they can understand discipline.

I think that one reason why so many people dislike the
idea of parental discipline is that they associate it with
cold, stern parents who beat their children often, but
never show them much love or affection. Discipline was
never intended to be the only contact between parents and
children: parents need to apply love as well as the rod.
Their love assures their children that the parents are basically pleased with them and care about their well being.
Parents should also show respect for their children as individuals and as fellow Christians. Insults, deliberate em-
barrassments, and put-downs damage a child's self-
esteem, and the child who feels worthless usually aban-
dons any effort to behave correctly.

When discipline is kept in the context of a loving relationship between parents and children, with the parents

showing affection and respect for their children, it can become an experience of love.

Setting Rules

One of the most common mistakes parents make when they discipline their children is inconsistency. If dad's boss yelled at him all day long, the kids get spanked the minute they step out of line. If he got a pay raise, he won't care if they tear the house apart. The confusion that such inconsistency creates totally undermines the purpose of discipline. Children do not learn to avoid wrong behavior; they just learn to avoid dad when he is in a bad mood. They also see the injustice of arbitrary spanking and begin to resent their parents' authority.

It is very important, then, that parents discipline not on the basis of their feelings, but according to consistent established rules. They should let their children know what types of misbehavior they will punish, and then follow through with the discipline consistently. Even when they don't feel like giving a spanking—they are tired or busy or don't want to bother—they owe it to their children to be consistent.

One obstacle to establishing consistent discipline is disagreement between the parents. When one parent spanks the children for things that the other parent ignores, the children end up with conflicting signals. Perhaps mom spanks them for tracking mud in, while dad could care less about muddy floors. Or dad spanks them for wrestling in the living room, but mom lets them get away with it. However the inconsistency appears, it destroys any effectiveness the discipline could have.

For the sake of consistency, then, the parents must be able to unite behind one policy for discipline. The father especially must show his support for whatever policy they decide on. Usually, mothers spend more time with the children and so end up dealing with discipline most often. But the letter to the Ephesians addresses *fathers* when it says, "Fathers, [raise your children] in the discipline and instruction of the Lord" (6:4). The father, as head of the family, is supposed to take active leadership in the discipline of his children. He cannot sit back with the newspaper and ignore his wife's efforts to keep the kids in line. He has to stand fully behind the discipline that his children receive. When he is home, he should normally administer any discipline.

When it comes to establishing a policy for discipline, I see two basic types of misbehavior that should be punished by spanking. First, direct disobedience toward parents. Children need to learn that their parents are in charge. If a parent gives a clear command, the child should obey or be disciplined.

Parents should be sure, however, that their clear commands are really clear. I know that at times I will ask my children, "Would you like to go upstairs and get dressed?" When they answer no, they've got me. I gave them the choice, and they exercised it. I may have intended to tell them, "Go get dressed, now," but I didn't. Parents have to speak clearly and communicate exactly what they want their children to do.

Ordinarily, parents should expect children to obey their first request. They should not keep repeating themselves while waiting for a response. Delays and stalling are often a form of disobedience, and can be treated as such. Of course, as children grow older they need more freedom to ask clarifying questions, offer their own opinions, add information, or even ask their parents to reconsider. But it should always be the parents who decide when discussion is in order and when the children should simply obey.

The second type of misbehavior that I recommend correcting with a spanking is a violation of any important rule made by the parents. For example, when a family lives on a busy street, the parents might tell their children not to leave the yard without permission. Once the children understand that a rule is established, they should be spanked any time they disobey.

Parents should make only those rules that are really necessary, especially when the children are small. Small children can understand, remember, and obey just so many instructions. Anything the parents can do to minimize rules in the home by baby-proofing the house or fencing the back yard or providing alternate activities will prove helpful. The whole family will be happier if mom just takes the breakable knick-knacks off the coffee table instead of making a rule about them.

Perhaps parents will find only two or three rules that their children can understand and that are important enough to be punished by spanking. Running into the street, or damaging other people's property, or hitting a younger brother or sister, could all be problems serious enough to warrant a spanking. A refusal to submit to discipline or direct disrespect would also be cause for spanking. When parents agree on a rule, they should tell the children what the rule is, why they have made it, and what punishment the children will receive if they break it. Children find it much easier to obey rules if they understand them, see the reasons behind them, and know that they will be enforced.

Many parents have told me that once they started using discipline consistently and fairly, their children really appreciated it. Children have an amazing capacity to see the justness of physical discipline when it is properly administered. A child who has done something wrong feels guilty, just as anyone else does, and wants some way to resolve the wrongdoing. Children recognize that discipline can do that.

One father has had his children come to him several times saying that they needed a spanking because they had lied, even though he had not caught them. They felt bad about lying and wanted to repent. I have had similar experiences with my children. Children want to face the fact that they have done wrong, resolve the wrongdoing, and be reconciled.

CHAPTER FIFTEEN

HOW TO DISCIPLINE

M any parents have never learned how to discipline their children. They may think, "What's there to learn? If you're going to spank your kids, just turn them over your knee and spank them." But spankings can be given either in a way that helps children resolve their wrongdoing and be reconciled with their parents or in a way that leaves them bitter and resentful. A great deal depends on the consistency of the discipline, but the actual way parents spank is also important. I would like to offer here a few guidelines for administering a spanking.

To begin with, spankings should usually be given immediately after the child is discovered misbehaving. This is particularly important with young children, who need to see a direct link between their behavior and the punishment. Even older children are helped by an immediate spanking, which resolves misbehavior at once rather than leaving the threat of punishment to hang over their heads for several hours.

A spanking should ordinarily be given in privacy to protect the child's dignity and self-respect. The humiliation of being disciplined in front of other people can be far more painful than the actual punishment. And unlike a spanking, this pain can damage the child's self-esteem and ability to relate to others. So if other people are present, the parent and child should go to a room where they can be alone. This is not always possible, but ordinarily the parent should try to administer discipline in privacy.

The actual spanking should be hard enough and long enough to hurt—say ten firm whacks instead of two or three little pats. The parent should not run any risk of injuring the child, of course, but the spanking should be painful enough that the child won't want it repeated. Otherwise, the whole purpose is defeated. I know parents who were spanking their children five or ten times a day without seeing any results. It turned out that they were giving the kids a few mild taps each time. The kids thought, "That doesn't hurt. They can spank me all they want." Many fewer spankings will be necessary if the children find them sufficiently unpleasant.

That leaves the question of what to spank with—the hand, a paddle, a wooden spoon, a belt? Some parents feel that since Scripture usually refers to the "rod" of discipline, parents should use only a rod or switch. They feel the hand should be used only for blessing and showing affection, not for spanking.

Personally, I do not think the authors of Scripture really meant to specify a particular instrument for spanking. I think the best criterion to follow in this matter is simply to find an instrument that will produce an unpleasant experience without injuring the child. A hand may be quite effective on a toddler's bare bottom, but it is less effective for a nine-year-old. My wife and I usually use either a belt or a paddle when spanking our children; we feel that these give an effective spanking without injury.

I occasionally hear people say that they try not to show any anger when spanking their children. Certainly, parents should not let themselves be so mastered by anger that they end up frightening or hurting their children. In fact, parents with really violent, uncontrollable tempers should leave spanking to their spouses until they learn how to control their anger. But I believe that parents can ordinarily let their children see that they are angry with disobedience or misbehavior. Anger, if properly controlled, helps children understand the seriousness of doing wrong. A parent who keeps up a facade of perfect peace and calm—"Oh my! That was wrong. I'll have to discipline you now, you know"—gives his child a false impression about the whole situation. If the offense has been outrageous, show a little outrage.

After the spanking is finished, many parents make the mistake of acting sorry about it—"Oh, you poor thing. Mommy and Daddy didn't mean it." That cancels out any lesson the spanking might have taught. All the child sees is that the parents feel guilty; naturally he wonders if he really deserved the spanking in the first place. Discipline is supposed to help children face the consequences of what they have done, and that cannot happen so long as parents try to keep their children in a lovey-dovey emotional haze.

Rather than start sympathizing, the parent should help the child understand the purpose and justness of the spanking. Parent and child can review the misbehavior being punished and recall what the child should have done in that situation. The child should then ask forgiveness from the parent for disobeying or misbehaving or whatever. If the child has injured another person in some way—say a little boy has thrown a rock at his sister—the child should ask forgiveness of that person as well.

When the child asks forgiveness, the parents should always say, "I forgive you. I love you." Children need to be assured the spanking really has resolved their wrongdoing and restored a good relationship with their parents. In families where discipline is not administered and children and parents do not repent and forgive, there gets to be a whole network of unresolved hurts and resentments and guilt and insecurities. The things that happen between parents and children, between brothers and sisters, are never resolved. Physical discipline, when followed by repentance and forgiveness, brings real freedom with it. A child can walk away from a spanking with joy and peace because he knows that he has turned from doing wrong and is at peace with his parents again.

Limitations of Spanking

Punishment by itself will not always resolve a child's behavior problems. While parents should normally punish wrong behavior under any circumstances, they may also need to deal with other factors if they want the problem fully resolved. For example, small children sometimes become so over-tired that they lose the ability to control their behavior. At such times, they may need to go to bed more than they need a spanking, and the parents' rules should allow enough freedom for this to happen.

Misbehavior may also signal some frustration or anxiety in a child's life. The wrong behavior itself should be punished, but the parents must also help the child deal with the frustration at its source.

We used to live near a Christian family with a nine-year-old son, Jeffrey. Our son John played with Jeffrey a lot, and despite their age difference, the two boys got along very well. At one point, however, both sets of parents noticed that Jeffrey was teasing John and treating him badly. Since he was disobeying his parents' rules for how to treat younger children, he was spanked.

After the spanking, however, Jeffrey's parents noticed that he seemed to be feeling some kind of frustration. A little probing revealed that he was having problems in school; his frustration there had provoked the mistreatment of John. This didn't excuse Jeffrey, but it did show his parents how to get to the root of his bad behavior. They talked to their son and his teacher to help clear up the school situation, and then John and Jeffrey were back on good terms.

Parents whose child has a physical, emotional or mental handicap must also take this factor into account when dealing with misbehavior. They should expect obedience and good behavior from their child, but they will need to make adjustments in their goals and means of communication according to the child's abilities.

Today parents worry so much about children's psyches that we are sometimes paralyzed by the fear of making a mistake that might damage their self-esteem or give them some kind of complex. But children are not too fragile to survive an occasional mistake. Any parent is going to end up giving an undeserved spanking or laying down a rule that proves to be unjust. In these cases, the parent should be willing to admit the mistake and ask the child's forgiveness, but they need not get excessively worried by the slip. Children will not be warped for life just because they had parents with human limitations.

Other Forms of Discipline

Spanking is the best discipline for correcting direct disobedience or violation of important family rules. Other forms of discipline may be more effective in reinforcing training or teaching.

Suppose, for example, a couple want to teach their children table manners. They usually begin by explaining what they want their children to do—"Say please when asking for the mashed potatoes" or "Don't eat spaghetti with your fingers." Over a period of time, they continue to explain and re-explain and give reminders. But finally a point comes when the children know perfectly well what the parents want, have had plenty of reminders, and need to start doing it.

When this point comes, the parents may need to use

some kind of discipline to back up their instructions. I would recommend using what I call "consequential discipline"—"If you don't do this, then this will follow."

Anne and I did have problems getting our daughter Mary Sarah to use table manners. For almost a year, night after night, we reminded her, "If you want something, say please." She was not responding. We finally decided to use some kind of discipline so that Mary Sarah could see we were serious about her manners. Spanking did not seem the best solution; instead, we told Mary Sarah that if she did not ask for something properly the first time, she would not get it.

The next time Mary Sarah asked us for another glass of milk without first saying please, she did not get it. This was a big shock. She did *not* like the experience of not getting what she wanted. Within a week she was saying please and thank you almost every time she asked for something. One week of consequential discipline accomplished what a whole year of reminders had failed to do. Later on we were able to allow her more flexibility: she did not have to use the precise word please as long as she asked politely. This type of discipline is effective with many common problems in children's behavior. Many a child has learned to eat his dinner because he could not have dessert unless he did.

Consequential discipline can also effectively correct misbehavior that is not serious enough to deserve a spanking. When he was three, my son John used to spend a lot of time with his cousin, also three. They loved to play together, but they also liked to contradict one another. One would say, "We're having peanut butter for lunch," and the other would say, "No we're not." One would say, "I'm three years old," and the other would answer, "No you're not. I'm three years old." This went on almost constantly, often until they started hitting each other or throwing toys.

The problem had to be corrected, so Anne and I and my

sister and her husband agreed to separate the boys for fifteen minutes whenever they started contradicting. That was real punishment, because they loved to play together and hated to be separated. We explained the new policy to the boys and began to enforce it. Soon they were spending their time together peacefully and happily, without the quarreling that had gone on before.

Consequential discipline also serves to supplement spanking when parents are punishing misbehavior serious enough to warrant more than a spanking. One couple I know had to punish their little girl for throwing rocks at the neighbor's car. Somehow she and one of her friends had decided to put dirt on the shiny new Cadillac next door. When caught, they were merrily pelting the car with gravel.

Though the car was not damaged, the parents wanted their daughter to learn how serious her misbehavior was. So besides spanking her, they took away her tricycle— which she had been riding at the start of the incident—for three days. They explained to her that they were doing this because throwing rocks at someone's car is wrong, and they wanted her to learn to do what is right. When three days were up, the little girl got back her tricycle, but she also told her parents that she had learned her lesson and was glad for it.

With older children, consequential discipline is especially useful. If a teenager doesn't come home from a party at the time agreed upon, she doesn't get to go the next time. If a twelve-year-old is out riding his bike when he is supposed to be mowing the lawn, his bike is taken away for several days. The older the child, the more important it is to explain the discipline clearly and give the reason for it. And the parents should be careful to see that the discipline does not become a cause of hidden resentment.

The same rules that apply to physical discipline apply to consequential discipline. The parents should agree on the punishment, they should explain it clearly to the children, and they should enforce it consistently. The discipline itself should be unpleasant enough to produce a change. A little boy will not be greatly impressed if he is told that he cannot brush his teeth unless he makes his bed. The discipline has to affect something the child likes to do.

The discipline should not be so tough that it either crushes the child or becomes impossible to enforce. Taking a child's toy away for three months or telling him that he can never go to so-and-so's house again is usually too much. A small child finds even a few days a very long time; usually a discipline has to last only a short while to be effective.

Verbal correction is another possible means of disciplining a child. Once a basic respect for the parents' authority has been established, it may only be necessary to say, "Harry, you know better than to leave your dirty clothes there," to correct misbehavior of that nature. Verbal correction is most appropriate when dealing with an occasional lapse by a usually responsible child or when dealing with older children who have a basically good relationship with the parents. Occasionally, even stronger verbal correction, which could be described as a "bawling out," could be in order.

As with all types of discipline, verbal correction is intended to change behavior. When children do not respond to it, the parents should not let themselves fall into mere nagging. They should consider other forms of discipline—possibly returning to spanking or finding an appropriate means of consequential discipline.

There is one other subject I want to mention briefly here, even though it is not actually a form of discipline. That is the use of rewards. Some authorities tell parents to reward their children for good behavior rather than punish them for bad behavior. I believe that children should learn to obey not because of the reward they will get, but because it is the right thing to do. Yet I also see a place for rewards in reinforcing certain kinds of training.

When parents are trying to teach their children some basic skill—how to tie shoes, for example—rewards can give the children a little more incentive to learn. If a child knows that he is going to get some special outing with his parents once he learns to tie his shoes, he will be much more eager to learn how to tie them. In such situations, the added incentive of a reward can be very helpful.

What Age Child Should Be Disciplined?

Many parents shy away from disciplining either a very small child or a teenager. They are sure that the one is too young to understand correction and the other too old for physical indignity. I myself would not necessarily recommend spanking infants or sixteen-year-olds, but neither would I set an arbitrary cut-off date for any type of discipline.

In general, I believe that some form of discipline should start at an early age. The proverb, "Discipline your son while there is hope" (Prov. 19:18), speaks of a critical formation period in children's lives that parents must take advantage of. The smallest infant is already learning how to respond to parents, to other children, to the world outside. As soon as a child is able to understand what the parents want, the need for discipline appears.

What age might this be? Nine months, a year, thirteen months, fourteen? The actual age varies with each child, but somewhere around that age children can understand that their parents don't want them to throw food on the floor or pull over the lamp. Once the child can understand that, the parents' authority is on trial.

"Susie, don't throw your food on the floor." Susie throws

her food down, and nothing happens except that mom or dad picks it up. Susie tries again, and again nothing happens. At this point Susie decides that mom and dad don't really mean what they say. If she wants to throw her food around, she can do it.

From a very early age, then, children are learning whether they really have to obey their parents. The discipline, or lack of discipline, they get is what teaches them. This is not to say that a nine-month-old girl should get a full-fledged spanking every time she throws her food around: often a slap on the hand or some type of consequential discipline, like taking the food away, is very effective. Nor should parents expect children of this age to obey automatically even after they are corrected. If little Jonathan starts to pull the lamp over, he may need to have his hand slapped, but he should also be removed from the lamp.

I would certainly not want to rule out spankings for younger children. I know one woman who spanked her seven-month-old daughter for crying and fighting when her diaper was changed. First, the mother checked to make sure that she was not hurting the baby in any way. Once she was sure the crying was unnecessary, she spent several days communicating that she wanted this behavior to stop by gently restraining her squirming daughter and saying no. When she was sure her daughter understood what she wanted, she began to spank her—giving her a few slaps on the bottom—whenever she fought. Within a couple of weeks, the problem was gone.

As a child grows older, the need for physical discipline usually diminishes. If parents have administered discipline while the children are young, their authority will be well established. Children will continue to need discipline as they go through adolescence, but if they already have a good basic relationship with their parents' authority, they will usually need only some type of consequential discipline rather than a spanking. As children grow up, the parents will finally stop using physical discipline completely.

Yet parents should not attempt to set an arbitrary age limit for physical discipline. I was recently talking with the principal of a Christian school. A seventeen-year-old girl who had just become a dedicated Christian began attending his school and was giving her teachers a hard time. One day when she was acting particularly badly, the principal felt that he should spank her, a discipline which the school policies permitted. He explained the policy of the school to her, took her to his office, and spanked her. The girl let out a big shriek and bawled her head off. But as she left his office, she told the secretary, "Did I ever need that!" From that day, her whole attitude toward her teachers changed for the better.

I do not propose this example as a helpful way to deal with all seventeen-year-olds. But I think the story shows that there are no hard and fast rules for when children become too old to be spanked. Some children reach a point where they no longer need much physical discipline when they are as young as nine or ten. Others don't reach that point until much later. The parents need to judge carefully what discipline is right for each child.

Parents who have not been disciplining their children as they grow up should be especially cautious about suddenly introducing physical discipline when the children are older. This is a very difficult situation in which the parents need special discernment and sensitivity to decide on a discipline that helps their children obey.

Before he left his disciples to return to the Father, Jesus promised that he would not leave them orphans. That is a promise which parents should remember whenever they feel unable to face the challenges of raising children. The Lord does not leave us when the children arrive; he is there to help us. When we face a difficult situation with the children, we must be able to turn to the Lord and ask him for understanding and guidance.

But besides his own counsel and guidance, Jesus left us with each other. We are not orphans because we have a whole family of Christian brothers and sisters to support us. As Christian parents, we need to drop our defensiveness about our families and learn to accept help from other mature Christians. Parents always seem to have at least one serious blind spot when it comes to understanding their own children and they need the insight of other Christians to guide them. Anne and I have worked very hard to understand our children and raise them properly, but some of the most important insights we have received for them have come from mature single people who knew our family well or from other parents who had already learned a lesson we needed. They were able to see things the Holy Spirit wanted to do with our children when we could not.

Christian parents should be looking for ways to draw together with their brothers and sisters to find counsel and support. Just having a few other Christian families to talk to and share experiences with is a great help. The Lord does not want each family to have to bear its burdens alone; he wants to give them brothers and sisters who can share those burdens.

The Lord has made each married couple the pastors of their family, with a serious responsibility to the children he has entrusted to them. He has given us the promise of his help. He has given us his word and counsel in Scripture. He offers us the support of other Christians. Parents need to accept all these supports, and then diligently apply themselves to loving and guiding their children.

Part Three

*Husbands, Wives,
Parents, Children*

CHAPTER SIXTEEN

THE FAMILY AND THE CHRISTIAN COMMUNITY

The main focus of this book has been the internal life of the Christian family. But at several points I have also mentioned the family's need for relationships outside itself in the larger Christian community. It would be misleading to conclude this book without explaining this point more fully. For the Christian family cannot achieve all it should unless it first finds its proper place in a wider context of committed Christian relationships.

Any study of the family's history will reveal that the family has never successfully functioned as a self-sufficient unit, cut off from the supports and services of a broader community. For Christians, that broader community is the "brethren"—our brothers and sisters in Christ. Unfortunately, many modern Christians only see these "brethren" on Sunday morning. They play no real part in raising one another's children, supporting one another's spiritual growth, or strengthening one another's marriages. Closer ties still exist in many smaller churches, in rural areas, and within ethnic neighborhoods, but the overwhelming majority of Catholic and Protestant churches do not offer their members that network of committed relationships that is genuine Christian community. Most Christians live in relative isolation, and their ability to live out their beliefs suffers accordingly.

Given this situation, one may realistically raise some questions in response to what I have written on the responsibilities of Christian husbands and wives. Can men really fulfill the role of Christian husband if they are not supported by other Christian men? Can Christian women find real joy in their role as wives if they receive no encouragement and help from other women? Will our children persevere in the faith without the witness and support of their peers and of other adults?

In many cases, the answer to these questions is no. Many people will find it extremely difficult to live the life of the Christian family without some degree of support from others living the same life. In fact, it is not uncommon to find Christian couples now who feel like failures because they have not been able to live up to the ideals of Christian family life. Despite all their efforts, they see the secular culture making steady inroads in their lives and the lives of their children.

If the renewal of the Christian family is to succeed on a large scale, it must be accompanied by an even wider renewal of the Christian community. There are unbreakable theological and practical connections that link these two entities. Scripture states that the family, especially the relationship between husband and wife, is a model of the relationship that exists between Christ and the church. The church, and its visible expression in the local community, is supposed to be a model of the unity God desires to effect over the entire earth: the family a sacrament to the church, the church a sacrament to the world.

John Chrysostom states that "a home is a little church." That basic insight was echoed in the Catholic Church when the Second Vatican Council referred to the family as a "domestic church." It is an insight rooted in the New Testament. Paul, for example, states that seeing considered for church leadership must "manage his own household well, keeping his children submissive and respectful in every way; for if a man does not know how to manage his own household, how can he care for God's church?" (1 Tim. 3:4-5). In the same letter, Paul refers to the local church as "the household of God" (1 Tim. 3:15).

To understand the full scope of God's plan for our lives, we need to examine the tremendously important ties between the family and the local Christian community. I would like to draw on what we have learned about the Christian family in order to give some principles for the life of the wider Christian community.

First of all, the local church should be a set of committed interpersonal relationships, like a family, rather than a purely administrative or educational institution. A family is based on a marriage covenant between two people and the Lord. In the same way, the life of the local church should be based on the members' covenant to the Lord and to one another. They become brethren, members of one another, forming a local body in which Christ dwells and acts, and through which he accomplishes his mission.

The members of a family are concerned not only with their individual well-being, but with the good of the whole family. In the same way, the members of a local parish or congregation should be concerned for one another's whole lives, helping each member of the body find his right place and receive the proper care.

The purpose of the marriage covenant that underlies family life is to make two people one flesh. Again in the same way, God's purpose in the local Christian community is to knit his people together in love and commitment, so that they form one new man, a single body with Christ as the head. Paul compares the Christian community to the human body, in which many separate parts work together as one: "For just as the body is one and has many members, and all the members of the body, though many, are one body, so it is with Christ ... God has so composed the body ... that there may be no discord in the body, but that the members may have the same care for one another. If one member suffers, all suffer together; if one member is honored, all rejoice together" (1 Cor. 12:12-26).

The keynote in such a community is cooperation rather than competition, faith rather than fear, sharing rather than greed, love rather than self-concern. In this way, all together give glory to God by showing forth the quality and nature of his life to the world.

When a family is truly united, people can see it; in the same way, the unity of the local community, if real, will be visible. Simply praying for one another or worshipping together is not enough. The lives of the members must be intermingled. Lawnmowers must be loaned, babysitting offered, houses painted, extra clothing shared, single parents assisted, single adults valued and cared for, teenagers guided, songs sung, sorrows shared, the sick visited and prayed for, talents used, and love and unity increased.

This is the pattern for church life we find at the very beginning of the church in Jerusalem. And as the Genesis account of creation provided us an insight into God's fundamental purposes for marriage, so the accounts of the Christian church's beginnings give us an insight into his fundamental purposes for the life of the church:

So those who received his word were baptized, and there were added that day about three thousand souls. And they devoted themselves to the apostles' teaching and fellowship, to the breaking of bread and the prayers. And fear came upon every soul; and many signs and wonders were done through the apostles. And all who believed were together and had all things in common; and they sold their possessions and goods and distributed them to all, as any had need. And day by day, attending the temple together and breaking bread in their homes, they partook of food with glad and generous hearts, praising God and having favor with all

the people. And the Lord added to their number day by
day those who were being saved.

(Acts 2:41-47)

The parallels between the structure and life of the family and the structure and life of the Christian community
could be fruitfully explored at greater length. For now, we
will consider only one more of these parallels—the paral-
lel nature and function of authority.

The family needs the clear establishment of loving authority and joyful subordination to achieve the unity of one
flesh. The local community also needs the loving authority
of the elders and the joyful subordination of the body. The
father in the family does not have a monopoly on gifts or
authority, nor do the elders of the local body. In the early
church, the elders shared their authority with the deacons
and deaconesses, encouraged the development and expression of each member's gifts, and coordinated the
working of the body as one unit. The responsibilities of
the elders were similar to the responsibilities of fathers of
families. That is why Paul told Timothy to choose the elders on the basis of how well a man fathered his own
family. As the father of the family shared in the fatherhood
of God, so did the elders of the community share in God's
fatherhood for his people.

A renewal of family life must be accompanied by a renewal of the life of the local Christian body, and vice-
versa, so profound is their relationship, so significant their
interdependence. The family, which is a cell of the larger
body of the local community, needs the local community
in order to be what it is called to be. Our families need the
help of brothers and sisters, the teaching, the encouragement, the contact with other husbands and wives, the
chance for children to form friendships with other Christian children, the community environment that makes it
possible to receive direction from God and have it tested,

the opportunity to be part of a people, for which we were destined.

The local community needs the family to form people in the Christian life by providing an atmosphere where Christ is followed and obeyed, where men and women act like men and women, where single members of the body can be befriended, where single parents can receive support, where guests can be received, where hospitality can be offered, where goods can be shared, where new Christians can be nurtured.

Sometimes a false opposition can arise between the individual family and the larger community. This often involves miscommunication or problems of time or schedule that can usually be worked out. The important fact is that the family needs the larger community and the community needs its smaller units, the families. In God's plan they were designed to function together and build each other up. God wants a people, a nation that he can call his own, who walk in his ways and show forth his nature in every aspect of their lives.

Granted that this is God's purpose for his people, what can we do to achieve it? The problem needs to be approached on two levels—that of the leadership of the Christian churches and that of the individual parent or family. Let me conclude by saying a few things about what we can do on each level.

First, the level of church leadership. Leaders of the Christian churches need to commit themselves to re-forming family life and the life of the local church body. This re-formation needs to be based on recognition of God's plan for the family and the local Christian community as found in Scripture, and a decision to settle for nothing less than that. For some leaders this will mean genuine repentance for unfaithfulness to God and his Word. For all leaders it will mean realizing that the Christian churches are in serious trouble, and that the solution needed is clearly beyond our human capabilities.

Something like an intervention of God is necessary if the vast numbers of nominally Christian families are to stay Christian or deepen their faith. Presently the Christian manpower to lead a genuine renewal is scarce. Few Christians are living according to God's plan in the life of families, functioning as cells of local church bodies that are actually functioning as bodies. The re-formation I described cannot be carried out by executive order, or by distributing program kits, or by putting articles in the denominational magazine. The hopes of it happening, humanly speaking, are dim. But when we turn to God, even the impossible becomes possible. God can raise up more leaders and give his power to those who already lead. No Christian leader, however, can expect to exercise truly effective leadership unless he himself undertakes to live the life he is calling his people to lead. This may mean a drastic personal change in lifestyle. Many Christian leaders lead more isolated, individualistic, and fragmented lives than their people. You cannot form or lead a community from outside it.

Nor can you build community without knowing what it is. Christian leaders who hope to do something useful about the present situation should be talking to people who know about the life of Christian families in communities, those who are themselves living these realities.

What about the level of the individual Christian and family?

Practically speaking, individuals, families, husbands, and wives should look for other people who want to open up their lives to God and grow together into God's plan as brothers and sisters in the Lord. A beginning step can be to discover a local bible study or prayer group of other Christians who want to grow in a common life. Sometimes such groups exist in a given parish or congregation, sometimes they do not. Sometimes they are composed of members of a single church body, sometimes they are ecumenical. Whatever shape they come in, finding a responsible and sound group of Christians who want to grow together in the Christian life can be an important practical step to take.

Some groups centered on prayer and Bible study grow on to develop many elements of committed Christian relationships and community life. Others do not. Sometimes families that want to commit themselves more fully to a community life have to move to a place where a Christian community is already established.

Whatever our own circumstances as regards Christian community, if we increasingly give our lives to God and to our brothers and sisters in Christ, the Lord will lead us in the right direction. Even if we end up in a situation that remains far from "ideal," we can trust that no effort we put into following and serving the Lord in our families and in the wider community will ever in his eyes be in vain.

CHAPTER SEVENTEEN

THE LIFE OF THE WORLD TO COME

A Christian couple in a distant city have come to a living relationship with the Lord and one another when their children are almost fully grown. They have little support from other Christians. Without that help, they don't seem able to lead their children into their new life.

A dedicated Christian woman was divorced before she came to a relationship with the Lord. She now has the pain of seeing the effects of the divorce on her children and the daily burden of raising them with only one parent.

A couple I know have been trying for years to overcome certain problems in their marriage, but have seen few results so far.

A woman whose husband of thirty years has died knows a loneliness that even the support of a Christian community cannot fully assuage.

Our second son, Mark, was born too soon and died a few minutes after birth.

Even when we do all we can to follow the Lord, we will not be spared suffering. Whether as a result of our own failings, the failings of others, or simply the sin of the fallen world, suffering is a part of life. The fevered bodies of sick children are not always healed; non-Christian husbands are not always converted; satisfactory communica-

tion is not always established; children do not always
choose for the Lord; deep sorrows are not always forgotten.

No matter how much of Christ's new life we are able to
live out, we and all creation still fall short of the full redemption that will be ours only when the Lord comes
again. " ... the dead will be raised imperishable, and we
shall all be changed. For this perishable nature must put
on the imperishable, and this mortal nature must put on
immortality" (1 Cor. 15:52-53). Then every tear will be
wiped from our eyes, and marriage and family life will find
their deepest fulfillment in the marriage feast of the Lamb.
We work hard now to apply God's wisdom to our families,
and we still see unresolved problems. We need to remember that "if for this life only we have hoped in Christ,
we are of all men most to be pitied" (1 Cor. 15:19).

We live at a time when redemption has appeared in its
initial flowering—the age of the church—but not in the
full fruit of the complete, eternal joy that will be ours
when Jesus comes again. Living as we are between the
first and second comings, we continue to experience the
wounds of the fallen creation. Sickness, accidents, natural
disasters, wars, and violent crimes break into our lives,
causing us grief and pain even though we also know the
goodness of the Lord.

Because we are Christians, we are not defenseless in the
face of the evil and suffering of this world. The Lord's
healing is available and active. We can experience his direct intervention in our difficulties. We have spiritual
power to combat the assaults Satan makes upon us. And
obedience to God protects us from much suffering that
would otherwise result from our sin.

Yet the world's suffering remains, and we as Christians,
as Christian families, do not stand apart from it. Scripture
says, "All creation groans and is in agony even until now.
Not only that, but we ourselves, although we have the

Spirit as first fruits, groan inwardly while we await the redemption of our bodies" (Rom. 8:22-23 NAB).

At times we cannot help but wonder why the Lord allows us to suffer. Scripture does not attempt to give a complete justification for every kind of suffering. It only assures us that "in everything God works for good with those who love him, who are called according to his purpose" (Rom. 8:28). In ways we do not always understand, God uses our sufferings to prepare us for glory. "This is a cause of great joy for you, even though you may for a short time have to bear being plagued by all sorts of trials; so that, when Jesus Christ is revealed . . . you will have praise and glory and honor" (1 Pet. 1:6-7 *Jerusalem Bible*).

Sometimes we can see God bringing good from our sufferings very clearly, almost immediately, as when a person misses a plane but meets an old friend because of the delay. We may see the Lord use suffering to make a perceptible difference in our character or personal strength. But God's full vindication of suffering, the full righting of every wrong, will not be effected until the day when we rise in Christ to everlasting life.

Christian family life has its ultimate hope in the world to come. As much as we love and receive love now, as much as we experience the joys of marriage and children, we know our marriages and families cannot give us complete and lasting happiness. Only God can do that. But we can taste that happiness within our families now, in a deepening anticipation of our eventual full union with the Lord. For a Christian family there is offered a joy, that in the midst of all and after all, Christ will triumph.

Yes, let's work hard to bring God's order into our lives and the lives of our families. Yes, let's work hard to raise our children in him. Let's work to improve our communication and sex life, to grow in unity, to learn about being husband and wife. But let's never forget that our goal in all of this is not "self-improvement," that the bond we seek is not the "pleasure bond." Our main concern is not to store up earthly treasure of any type—financial, physical, psychological—but to lay up treasure in heaven.

I would like to close with words which John Chrysostom pictured a husband addressing to his wife, words that express well the eternal perspective needed in Christian marriage:

> For this reason then, I courted you, and I love you and prefer you to my own soul. For the present life is nothing. And I pray and beseech, and do all I can, that we may be counted worthy so to live this present life, as that we may be able also there in the world to come to be united to one another in perfect security. For our time here is brief and fleeting. But if we shall be counted worthy by having pleased God to so exchange this life for that one, then shall we ever be both with Christ and with each other, with more abundant pleasure.

APPENDIX

An interesting commentary on marriage and family life is contained in St. John Chrysostom's sermon on Ephesians 5:22-24 (Homily 20 on Ephesians). John Chrysostom was bishop of Constantinople in the fifth century and is one of the great fathers of the church. I discovered the sermon while writing my book, and felt that many couples would find Chrysostom's insights both interesting and enjoyable. The following appendix contains a number of extracts from the sermon, which have been adapted from the translation found in vol. 13 of *A Select Library of the Nicene and Post-Nicene Fathers of the Christian Church* (reprinted in 1969 by Wm. E. Eerdman's, Grand Rapids, Michigan).

On Marriage

There is no relationship between man and man so close as that between man and wife if they be joined together as they should be.

Why does Paul say, "Wives, submit to your husbands as to the Lord"? Because when they are in harmony, the children are well brought up, and their household is in good order, and neighbors and friends and relations enjoy the fragrance. But if it be otherwise, all is turned upside down, and thrown into confusion. And just as when the generals of an army are at peace one with another, all things are in due subordination, whereas on the other hand, if they are at variance, everything is turned upside down; so, I say, is it also here. That is why he says "Wives, submit to your husbands as to the Lord."

For if partaking of the same table produces unanimity even in robbers toward their foes . . . ; much more will the becoming one flesh—for such is the being the partner of the bed—be effectual to draw us together.

If we seek the things that are incorruptible, the corruptible things will follow. "Seek first his kingdom, and all these things shall be added unto you" (Matt. 6:33). What sort of persons, think you, must the children of such parents be? What the servants of such masters? What all others who come near them? Will not they too eventually be loaded with blessings out of number? If thus we regulate ourselves, and attentively study the Scriptures, in most things we shall derive instruction from them. And thus shall we be able to please God, and to pass through the whole of the present life virtuously, and to attain those blessings which are promised to those that love him.

Advice to Husbands

You have seen the measure of (the wife's) obedience, hear also the measure of love. Would you have your wife obedient to you, as the Church is to Christ? Then take the same provident care for her as Christ takes for the Church. Yes, even if you must give your life for her, yes, and be cut into pieces ten thousand times, yes, and endure and undergo any suffering whatever—refuse it not. . . .

The partner of one's life, the mother of one's children, the foundation of one's every joy, one ought never to chain down by fear and menaces, but with love and good temper. For what sort of union is that, where the wife trembles at her husband? And what sort of pleasure will the husband himself enjoy if he dwells with his wife as with a slave, and not as with a free-woman? Yes, though you should suffer anything on her account, do not upbraid her: for neither did Christ do this.

Let us seek in a wife affectionateness, modest-mindedness, gentleness; these are the characteristics of beauty. But loveliness of person let us not seek, nor upbraid her upon these points, over which she has no power, nay, rather let us not upbraid at all, (it were rudeness) nor let us be impatient, nor sullen. Do you not see how many, after living with beautiful wives, have ended their lives pitiably, and how many, who have lived with those of no great beauty, have run on to extreme old age with great enjoyment. Let us wipe off the "spot" that is within, let us smooth the "wrinkles" that are within, let us do away with the "blemishes" that are on the soul. Such is the beauty God requires. Let us make her fair in God's sight, not in our own. Let us not look for wealth, nor for that high birth which is outward, but for that true nobility which is in the soul.

As great a love as each entertains toward himself, so great the Lord would have us entertain toward a wife. Not because we partake of the same nature; no, this ground of duty toward a wife is far greater than that; it is that there are not two bodies, but one; he the head, she the body.

"But what" one may say, "if a wife reverence me not?" Never mind, you are to love, fulfill your own duty. For though that which is due from others may not follow, we ought of course to do our duty .... What if another not submit himself? Still you obey the law of God ... Let the husband, though his wife does not reverence him, still show her love, that he himself be not wanting in any point. For each has received his own.

Paul took that former argument, the example of Christ, to show that we ought not only to love, but also to govern ... for if you shall make her "holy and without blemish," everything else will follow ... Govern your wife, and thus will the whole house be in harmony.

If we thus regulate our own houses, we shall be also fit for the management of the Church. For indeed a house is a little church.

Show your wife that you set a high value on her company, and that you are more desirous to be at home for her sake, than in the marketplace. And esteem her before all your friends, and above the children that are born of her, and let these very children be beloved by you for her sake. If she does any good act, praise and admire it; if any foolish one, ... advise her and remind her ... and be continually teaching her the things that are profitable.

Let your prayers be common. Let each go to Church; and let the husband ask his wife at home, and she again ask her husband, the account of things which were said and read there. If any poverty should overtake you, cite the case of those holy men, Paul and Peter, who were more honored than any kings or rich men; and yet how they spent their lives, in hunger and in thirst. Teach her that there is nothing in life that is to be feared, save only offending against God. If any marry thus, with these views, he will be but little inferior to monks; the married but little below the unmarried.

Teach her these lessons, but with much graciousness. For since the recommendation of virtue has in itself much that is stern ... whenever discourse on true wisdom are to be made, contrive that your manner be full of grace and kindness.

And above all banish this notion from her soul of "mine and yours." If she say the word "mine," say to her "What things do you call your own? For in truth I know not; I for my part have nothing of my own. How can you speak of 'mine' when all things are yours? ... If I have no power over my body (1 Cor. 7:4), but you have, much more do you have all my possessions. Even I am yours."

Honor her and she will not need honor from others; she will not want the glory that comes from others, if she enjoys that which comes from you. Prefer her before all, on every account, both for her beauty and her discernment, and praise her. You will thus persuade her to give heed to none that are without, but to scorn all the world except yourself. Teach her the fear of God, and all good things will flow from this as from a fountain, and the house will be full of ten thousand blessings.

Advice to Wives

When you obey your husband, do so as serving the Lord. For if he who resists the external authorities, those of governments, "withstands the ordinance of God" (Rom. 13:2), much more does she who submits not herself to her husband. Such was God's will from the beginning.

Let us take as our fundamental position that the husband occupies the place of the "head" and the wife the place of the "body." Let the wife fear and reverence her husband. The wife is a second authority; let her not then demand equality in authority for she is under the head; nor let him despise her as being in submission, for she is the body;

and if the head despise the body, it will itself also perish. But let him bring in love on his part as a counterpoise to obedience on her part. For example, let the hands and the feet, and all the rest of the members be given up for service to the head, but let the head provide for the body, seeing it contains every sense in itself. Nothing can be better than this union.

How can there ever be love, one may say, where there is fear and reverence? It will exist there, I say, preeminently. For she that fears and reverences, loves also; and she that loves, fears and reverences him as being the head, and loves him as being a member, since the head itself is a member of the body at large. Hence he places the one in submission and the other in authority that there may be peace; for where there is equal authority there can never be peace; neither where a house is a democracy, nor where all are rulers; but the ruling power must of necessity be one.

The wife, though seeming to be the loser in that she was charged to fear, is the winner, because the principal duty, love, is charged upon the husband.

Of what nature is the "fear" or "reverence" a wife should show her husband? It is the not contradicting, the not rebelling, the not being fond of the preeminence.

If you have a mind to give dinners, and to make entertainments, let there be nothing immodest, nothing disorderly. If you should find any poor saint able to bless your house, able only just by setting his foot in it to bring in the whole blessing of God, invite him.

Let your bedroom be handsome, still let not what is handsome degenerate into finery. No, leave these things to the people of the stage. Adorn your house yourself with all possible neatness, so as rather to breathe an air of soberness than much perfume.

INDEX